Scrumptious
# Cupcakes
for all Occasions

# Scrumptious Cupcakes
## for all Occasions

KATHRYN HAWKINS

JOHN BEAUFOY PUBLISHING

This edition first published in the United Kingdom in 2013 by
John Beaufoy Publishing, 11 Blenheim Court, 316 Woodstock Road,
Oxford OX2 7NS, England
www.johnbeaufoy.com

10 9 8 7 6 5 4 3 2 1

Copyright © 2011, 2013 John Beaufoy Publishing Limited
Copyright © 2011, 2013 in text and photographs John Beaufoy Publishing Limited
Copyright © 2011 in photographs Stuart MacGregor (except cover and p. 30)

All rights reserved. No part of this publication may be reproduced, stored in a retrieval system or transmitted in any form or by any means, electronic, mechanical, photocopying, recording or otherwise, without the prior written permission of the publishers and copyright holders.

Great care has been taken to maintain the accuracy of the information contained in this work. However, neither the publishers nor the author can be held responsible for any consequences arising from the use of the information contained therein.

ISBN 978-1-909612-03-7

Project manager: Rosemary Wilkinson
Design: Glyn Bridgewater
Photography: Stuart MacGregor (except p. 30, Ian Garlick)
Illustration: Stephen Dew

Printed and bound in Malaysia by Times Offset (M) Sdn. Bhd.

## RECIPE NOTES

- Whole milk has been used throughout. Other (reduced fat) milks can be used but the texture may differ.
- All eggs are medium unless otherwise stated.
- All spoon measurements are level unless otherwise stated.
- Metric and imperial measurements are not always exact equivalents, so only follow one set of measurements within each recipe.
- Oven temperatures have been given for conventional electric and gas ovens. For fan ovens, use the following equivalents:

| Electricity °C | Electricity (fan) °C |
| --- | --- |
| 110 | 90 |
| 120 | 100 |
| 130 | 110 |
| 140 | 120 |
| 150 | 130 |
| 160 | 140 |
| 170 | 150 |
| 180 | 160 |
| 190 | 170 |
| 200 | 180 |
| 220 | 200 |

# Contents

Introduction 6

1 Classics 16
2 Indulgence 36
3 Wholesome 56
4 Celebrations 76

Recipe index & acknowledgements 96

# Getting started

Muffins and cupcakes are very easy to make. This is the book that will give you ideas to suit all occasions and tastes, from the everyday teatime treat, to something more substantial for breakfast or supper, to the overtly indulgent for someone or something very special. You don't need much to get started, so read on.

### Muffin or cupcake?

Both cakes contain four basic ingredients: flour, sugar, egg and fat. What makes them different is the proportions of ingredients used as well as the method for making them. A muffin is a deep, airy cake creation, dense or light in texture depending on the ingredients used, and derived from a thick batter mixture. Traditionally served without icing, they can be sweet or savoury. They are baked in large paper cake cases set inside large cup muffin tins.

Cupcakes probably got their name from the fact that their ingredients were measured in cups rather than weighed, and that they were baked in cups or small basins to make individual sized cakes. They are, in fact, still made in small cases and tins. The texture is more sponge-like and softer than a muffin; they are made by creaming the butter and sugar together and lend themselves perfectly to being embellished in lavish ways with numerous types of topping, frosting, icing and decorations.

# Basic ingredients

**Butter and alternatives:** Dairy butter gives a rich flavour and texture to your baking but you may prefer to use a specific baking margarine for a lighter texture and flavour. You can use dairy-free versions for vegans or special diets and some methods call for vegetable oils instead of solid fat, giving a moist, rich texture to the sponge.

**Sugar and alternatives:** Refined white sugar dissolves quickly in cooking helping to give a lightness to the cooked sponge texture; it offers sweetness without other flavour. Brown and other unrefined sugars make the texture denser and give a caramel-richness to the mixture. You'll also find recipes using honey and maple syrup as alternatives to granular sweeteners.

**Flours:** Classic muffin and cupcake recipes call for white wheat flour, either plain or with added raising agent (self-raising). But for anyone with a wheat intolerance, you could replace the wheat flour with a gluten-free plain flour of your choice or use rice, potato or soya flour. Each variety will add its own unique flavour and texture to your baking. For all flours other than self-raising varieties, you'll need to add your own raising agents to the mixture as well – see below.

**Eggs:** Eggs help bind mixtures together. In cupcake mixtures, more eggs are used to help achieve a lighter, richer sponge. For best results, use good quality, fresh, free-range or organic eggs – the yolks will be richer giving colour and more flavour. Whilst eggs should be stored in the fridge, they are best used at room temperature. All recipes in this book use 'Medium' or 'Size 3' eggs unless otherwise stated.

**Raising agents:** A cake mixture made with a self-raising flour will be light, soft and have small, fine air bubbles. A cake made with unleavened flour plus a raising agent will be spongier in texture with larger air pockets. Which you prefer is down to personal taste. You'll find recipes in this book for both types. The most common raising agent is baking powder, which is a mixture of alkaline and acid substances. When moistened the powder produces a gas, which makes the mixture rise. Bicarbonate of soda (baking soda) is alkaline only and is used in a recipe which also contains an acid ingredient, such as buttermilk or lemon juice, in order to activate it. Cream of tartar is a mild acid-forming agent that mixes with bicarbonate of soda to make baking powder; it is used on its own to add volume to egg whites. Always use measuring spoons for accuracy and bake the mixture as soon as you can after "activating" the raising agent otherwise the gas will soon be lost.

**Milk and alternatives:** Muffin batter requires a quantity of liquid in order to bind the ingredients together; cupcake mixtures use more eggs so require little or no extra liquid. Dairy milk is the most frequently used liquid as it is mildly flavoured and adds a little extra richness due to its fat content but soya milk can be used as a dairy alternative, as can other dairy substitutes. Be mindful of any extra sweetness that these liquids may contain as this can affect the finished result; choose unsweetened varieties in preference. Also remember that the more fat a liquid contains, the denser the baked mixture will be, and the rise will be less 'spongy'.

## Other ingredients

In order to make your bakes individual, delicious extras are added to the basic mixtures. Chocolate is probably the number one favourite addition and you'll see recipes using cocoa powder, different varieties of whole chocolate for melting, as well as chips and chunks. Dried and fresh fruit, nuts and seeds are also popular additions. Flavourings such as vanilla, almond and coffee add their own distinct flavour note to a recipe – choose the best quality you can afford for the best results – and other ingredients such as citrus zest, herbs and spices and flower waters add an extra special zing to a mixture. Make

sure all flavourings are fresh for maximum impact on your taste buds.

## Basic methods

Whisked sponge: This uses egg whites. Crucially, you must whisk the separated egg whites in a clean, grease-free bowl in order to achieve a stiff, foamy whip for maximum rise. Eggs perform better when at room temperature. Sift the dry ingredients into the bowl in order to aerate them, then gently combine the dry ingredients with the whipped egg using a large metal spoon and a slow, slicing, "figure of eight" stirring motion. This too will ensure maximum air retention and a good rise.

Creamed sponge: This is the most common method for cupcakes. Use softened butter or margarine and beat it with the sugar or sweetening agent until it becomes paler, creamy and fluffy in texture. This means the sugar has begun to dissolve and that air has been  trapped to enable a good rise. Eggs are used as binding agents in this type of sponge so are simply whisked in. Dry ingredients should then be sieved in and the ingredients combined as described above.

All-in-one: This is a quick version of a creamed sponge that can be used to save time. Follow a standard cupcake recipe but put all the ingredients in the bowl at the beginning. Then using a hand whisk, beat the ingredients together until well combined. This type of mixture can benefit from an extra $1/2$ tsp of baking powder as well as the self-raising flour to guarantee a good rise. The texture of this type of sponge is less soft and light but still perfectly acceptable, and well worth an experiment if time is short.

**Batter:** Most traditional muffins are made from a thick batter. The dry ingredients are put in the bowl first (sieved where necessary); an indent is made in the centre and the egg, liquid and melted fat are poured into it. The ingredients are simply combined by a quick stir. Over mixing will give a tougher, chewier texture, so don't waste time trying to get everything perfectly blended. Batters usually contain less fat and use plain flours with additional raising agents. Their texture is well risen, light and aerated.

## Basic equipment

### Measuring scales, spoons and jug:
Accurate kitchen scales are important for large quantities, measuring spoons are vital for small amounts – always use a level measurement unless otherwise stated. Measuring jugs and spoons are also important for liquids.

**Sieve:** Not only important for getting rid of lumps, sieving fine ingredients like flour will help trap air in a mixture and thus lighten the texture of the finished bake. A small sieve (or tea strainer) is useful for dusting icing sugar on top as a finishing touch.

**Whisks:** For convenience and an excellent result, an electric hand mixer will give you the best result for a sponge in the minimum amount of time. Hand whisks can be used instead but are slower. For muffins, you don't need anything other than a wooden spoon!

Tins and moulds: If you get the baking bug, it is a worthwhile investment to purchase good quality, heavy gauge metal cookware. This doesn't warp or bend in the heat of the oven and will give you a good steady base for cooking. Bun and muffin tins have 6, 9 or 12-cup indentations. Non-stick bakeware means you can simply bake your mixture directly in the tin but most people prefer to use paper baking cases – see below. Traditionally, shallower bun tins are used to make smaller cakes like Fairy Cakes, whilst deeper muffin tins produce large cupcakes and are, of course, used for muffins. Mini cake tins are also available. For a longer term investment, you'll find reusable, ovenproof, dishwasher proof, silicone baking cases in bright or pastel colours. They are easy to use and you don't even need to put paper cases in them. Individual silicone cases can simply be placed on a baking sheet, then filled with cake mixture.

Cake cases: Available from cookshops and supermarkets or online in a huge range of sizes, colours and patterns.

If you want to be economical (or individual) you can make your own cases. It is best to use greaseproof paper, waxed paper or baking parchment but you can experiment with brown paper, wrapping paper and doyleys. Line non-culinary use papers with greaseproof as well and

avoid any paper with strong coloured dyes or glues as these may melt and seep through into your mixture. Cut out sufficient rounds of paper using a saucer or CD as a template. Find a tumbler or bottle that fits snugly into the cup indentations of your bun or muffin tin. Place a paper circle on top of each cup compartment and push the bottle down to press the paper into the tin and create a paper case. Make sure the papers are neatly creased flat against the cup sides to ensure an even finish. Use 10 cm/4 in squares of paper for a pointed edged case and, if liked, trim the edges with pinking shears.

Size note: The recipes in this book state which size tin and case to use for best results. The amount of mixture you put in a cake case or tin will affect the size of the finished cake and also the cooking time. Tins and cases are defined as very large (tulip-style cases which stand inside muffin tins), large (muffin), standard (traditional bun size) and mini (small).

## Baking and storing tips

Spoon cake mixture into your cases or tins using a small spoon and try to be as neat as possible. Each case should be $2/3$ full unless otherwise stated and the top of the mixture smoothed to give an even rise.

Oven temperatures will vary depending on the age, make and model of your cooker, so it is always a good idea to check to see if your cakes or muffins are cooked a few minutes before the stated time. Use the oven timer or a kitchen timer for accurate baking timing.

Put cake trays on the middle shelf for even cooking – swap trays round halfway through cooking time if you are batch baking; you may end up having to add extra baking time if you do this.

To test for "doneness", cakes should be lightly golden, gently peaked and just firm on top when touched lightly with your finger. A wooden cocktail inserted into the centre of a cake is the perfect indicator: if it comes out clean, the cakes are cooked. Once cooked, cool in the tin for a few minutes then transfer to a wire rack to cool completely.

Sponge cakes with a good fat content will keep in an airtight container for 4 to 5 days. Low-fat sponges and muffins are best eaten on the day they are baked. For best results, store all cakes uniced, then decorate just before serving. Cupcakes and muffins freeze well (unless otherwise stated) and can be frozen, without icing, in freezer bags or containers for up to 3 months. They are best thawed in their wrappings for an hour or so at room temperature.

## Decoration and finishing techniques

When it comes to serving up your freshly baked creations, the icing world is your oyster. Muffins are often served warm, just as they are or with a simple dusting of icing sugar on top. Cupcakes are usually more lavish and can be topped with anything from a simple water and icing sugar drizzle to a huge pile of whipped cream, soft cheese or buttercream icing. For a casual finish, simply spoon over your chosen topping; a swirl from a small palette knife will give a smooth, more rounded finish. If you want something more fancy, reusable or disposable piping bags fitted with a large star nozzle will help you pipe a generous a swirl of cream or icing on top. Disposable bags also give you the option of not using a  nozzle and just snipping off a specific amount of bag to give an outlet for piping more intricate detail. If you don't have readymade bags, you can make your own by putting your topping in a clean food bag. Squeeze it down towards one corner; get rid of the air and seal the bag in your hand, then carefully snip of the end to make a pointed outlet for piping through.

As well as natural decorations, such as fresh fruit, herbs and fruit zest, there's a myriad reasonably priced, coloured and shaped sugar sprinkles, piped sugar decorations like flowers and hearts, and chocolate bits and pieces you can use to add your own personal touches to your cakes. For something special, you'll find edible metallic balls, coloured shimmering glitter, clear sugar 'diamonds' and edible gold and silver leaf for adding a touch of luxury.

Ready-to-roll fondant icing is available in white or pre-coloured and can easily be rolled and cut or stamped using  pastry cutters to make your own shapes and unique decorations. Simply leave the shapes to dry on baking paper for a few hours before transferring to your cake tops – details can be painted onto the icing shapes using food colourings or piped on with icing.

introduction 15

I

# classics

Makes 9
Prep time: 15 mins
Cook time: 22-25 mins

225 g/8 oz plain flour
2 tsp baking powder
115 g/4 oz caster sugar

175 g/6 oz prepared fresh blueberries
1 egg, beaten
115 g/4 oz butter or margarine, melted
150 ml/5 fl oz whole milk
1 tsp pure vanilla extract

# Blueberry muffins

1 Line a 9-hole muffin pan with large paper cases. Preheat the oven to 190°C/375°F/Gas 5.

2 Sift the flour and baking powder into a mixing bowl, then stir in the sugar and blueberries. Make a well in the centre.

3 In a measuring jug, mix together the egg, melted butter or margarine, milk and vanilla extract. Pour into the well and mix lightly to form a thick rough batter.

4 Spoon into the muffin cases and bake for 22–25 minutes, until risen and golden. Transfer to a wire rack to cool. Best served warm.

classics

Makes 8
Prep time: 15 mins
Cook time: 25–28 mins

300 g/10 oz plain flour
1 tbsp baking powder
50 g/2 oz cocoa powder
115 g/4 oz light brown sugar, free of lumps
150 g/5 oz white, milk or plain chocolate chips
2 eggs, beaten
115 g/4 oz butter or margarine, melted
200 ml/7 fl oz whole milk

# Double chocolate muffins

1 Line an 8-hole muffin pan with very large paper cases. Preheat the oven to 190°C/375°F/Gas 5.

2 Sift the flour, baking and cocoa powders into a mixing bowl, then stir in the sugar and chocolate chips. Make a well in the centre.

3 In a measuring jug, mix together the eggs, melted butter or margarine and the milk. Pour into the well and mix lightly to form a thick rough batter.

4 Spoon into the muffin cases and bake for 25–28 minutes until risen and just firm to the touch. Transfer to a wire rack to cool.

TIP
Use your favourite chocolate in this mixture or replace the chocolate chips with small pieces of dried fruit.

Makes 10
Prep time: 15 mins
Cook time: 25–28 mins

350 g/12 oz plain flour
1 tsp bicarbonate of soda
115 g/4 oz caster sugar
200 g/7 oz sultanas
2 eggs, beaten
115 g/4 oz butter or margarine, melted
150 ml/5 fl oz buttermilk
finely grated zest of 1 unwaxed lemon
100 ml/3$^1/_2$ fl oz freshly squeezed lemon juice
10 pieces pared lemon zest

# Lemon and sultana muffins

1 Line a 10-hole muffin pan with very large paper cases. Preheat the oven to 190°C/375°F/Gas 5.

2 Sift the flour and bicarbonate of soda into a mixing bowl, then stir in the sugar and sultanas. Make a well in the centre.

3 In a measuring jug, mix together the egg, melted butter or margarine, buttermilk, lemon zest and juice. Pour into the well and mix lightly to form a thick rough batter.

4 Spoon into the muffin cases and place a piece of lemon zest on top. Bake for 25–28 minutes, until risen and golden. Transfer to a wire rack to cool completely.

**TIP**
For a flavour twist, replace lemon with orange zest and juice and use chopped, dried apricots instead of sultanas. Use a vegetable peeler to thinly pare off shavings of lemon zest for extra flavour and decoration.

Makes 12
Prep time: 20 mins
Cook time: 22–25 mins

400 g/14 oz plain flour
100 g/3½ oz butter or margarine
75 g/2½ oz + 1 tbsp caster sugar

1 tbsp baking powder
2 tsp ground cinnamon
2 eggs, beaten
150 ml/5 fl oz non-concentrated fresh apple juice
6 tbsp chunky apple sauce

# Spiced apple sauce streusel muffins

1 Line a 12-hole muffin pan with large paper cases. Preheat the oven to 200°C/400°F/Gas 6.

2 Sift 50 g/2 oz of the flour into a bowl and rub in 25 g/1 oz of the butter or margarine to form a crumbly topping. Stir in 1 tbsp of the sugar and set aside. Melt the remaining butter or margarine.

3 Sift the remaining flour along with the baking powder and cinnamon into another bowl, then stir in the remaining sugar. Make a well in the centre.

4 In a measuring jug, mix together the eggs and melted butter or margarine with the apple juice and sauce. Pour into the well and mix lightly to form a thick rough batter.

5 Spoon into the muffin cases. Sprinkle the tops lightly with the crumble mix and bake for 22–25 minutes, until risen and lightly golden. Transfer to a wire rack to cool. Best served warm.

Makes 12
Prep time: 25 mins plus setting
Cook time: 16–18 mins

115 g/4 oz butter or baking margarine, softened
115 g/4 oz caster sugar
2 eggs, beaten
115 g/4 oz self-raising flour

ICING
175 g/6 oz icing sugar
assorted food colourings (optional)
sugar flowers, to decorate

# Fairy cupcakes

1 Line a 12-hole cupcake pan with standard-size paper cases. Preheat the oven to 190°C/375°F/Gas 5.

2 In a mixing bowl, beat together the butter or margarine with the sugar until pale and creamy-light in texture.

3 Gradually whisk in the eggs, then sift the flour on top. Using a large metal spoon, carefully fold the flour into the batter.

4 Spoon into the cake cases and bake for 16–18 minutes until lightly golden and just firm to the touch. Transfer to a wire rack to cool completely.

5 To ice, sift the icing sugar into a bowl and gradually mix in sufficient warm water to make a smooth, spreadable icing. If using food colourings, divide into smaller bowls and mix in a few drops of your favourite shades.

TIP
For Chocolate Fairy Cakes, replace 15 g/1/2 oz of flour with cocoa powder and replace 15 g/1/2 oz icing sugar with cocoa powder to make a chocolate-flavoured icing.

6 Carefully spread the icing over each cake to cover, and decorate with sugar flowers. Allow to set for about 30 minutes before serving.

classics 27

Makes 12
Prep time: 25 mins
Cook time: 16–18 mins

75 g/2½ oz butter or baking margarine, softened
50 g/2 oz crunchy peanut butter
115 g/4 oz caster sugar
2 eggs, beaten
100 g/3½ oz self-raising flour
15 g/½ oz cocoa powder
100 g/3½ oz milk or plain chocolate chips

TOPPING
125 g/4½ oz full-fat soft cheese
125 g/4½ oz chocolate spread, softened
40 g/1½ oz peanut brittle, crushed

# Peanut butter and chocolate cupcakes

1 Line a 12-hole cupcake pan with standard-size paper cases. Preheat the oven to 190°C/375°F/Gas 5.

2 In a mixing bowl, beat together the butter or margarine and peanut butter with the sugar until pale and creamy-light in texture.

3 Gradually whisk in the eggs, then sift the flour and cocoa powder on top. Add the chocolate chips, then, using a large metal spoon, carefully fold the flour and chips into the batter.

4 Spoon into the cake cases and bake for 16–18 minutes until lightly risen and just firm to the touch. Transfer to a wire rack to cool.

5 For the topping, put the soft cheese in a bowl and beat until softened. Add the chocolate spread and gently mix together to give a marbled effect.

6 Just before serving, spread each cupcake thickly with the chocolaty soft cheese and sprinkle with peanut brittle.

Makes 12
Prep time: 25 mins
Cook time: 16–18 mins

1 quantity Fairy Cupcake mixture, see page 27
25 g/1 oz ground almonds
50 g/2 oz glacé cherries, chopped
1 tsp pure almond extract

TOPPING
icing sugar, to dust
125 g/4½ oz marzipan
4 tbsp cherry jam
fresh cherries, washed, to decorate (see TIP)

# Cherry almond cupcakes

1 Line a 12-hole cupcake pan with standard-size paper cases. Preheat the oven to 190°C/375°F/Gas 5.

2 Make up the Fairy Cupcake mixture, see steps 2 and 3 on page 27, then stir in the ground almonds, chopped cherries and almond extract.

3 Spoon into the cake cases and bake for 16–18 minutes until risen and lightly golden, and just firm to the touch. Transfer to a wire rack to cool.

4 Dust the work surface lightly with icing sugar and roll out the marzipan thinly. Using a 5 cm/2 in fluted round cutter, stamp out 12 rounds, re-rolling as necessary.

5 Spoon cherry jam onto each cake and lay a circle of marzipan on top. Decorate each with a fresh cherry.

TIP
To sugar-dip fresh cherries, brush with lightly whisked egg white, then dip in caster sugar. Allow to dry for a few minutes on baking parchment.

Makes 10
Prep time: 25 mins
Cook time: 16–18 mins

115 g/4 oz butter or baking margarine, softened
115 g/4 oz caster sugar
1 tsp pure vanilla extract
2 eggs, beaten

115 g/4 oz plain flour
1 1/2 tsp baking powder

ICING
75 g/2 1/2 oz unsalted butter, softened
150 g/5 oz icing sugar + 1 tsp
1/2 tsp pure vanilla extract
assorted food colourings (optional)
short thin lengths of candied peel or angelica, to decorate

# Butterfly cupcakes

1 Line a 10-hole cupcake pan with standard-size paper cases. Preheat the oven to 190°C/375°F/Gas 5.

2 In a mixing bowl, beat the butter with the sugar until pale and creamy-light in texture. Stir in the vanilla extract. Gradually whisk in the eggs, then sift the flour and baking powder on top and carefully fold into the batter.

3 Spoon into the cake cases and bake for 16–18 minutes until risen, lightly golden and just firm to the touch. Transfer to a wire rack to cool.

4 For the icing, place the butter in a bowl and beat until soft. Sift and beat in 150 g/5 oz of the icing sugar until smooth. Add vanilla to flavour. If using food colourings, divide into smaller bowls and mix in a few drops. Set aside.

5 Cut a circle off the top of each cake and cut in half. Spread half the icing onto the cakes. Put the rest in a piping bag filled with a 1 cm/ 1/2 in plain nozzle and pipe down the centre of each cake. Arrange 2 half circles on top to resemble wings. Dust with 1 tsp icing sugar and decorate with peel or angelica.

Makes 8
Prep time: 25 mins
Cook time: 22–25 mins

1 quantity Butterfly Cupcake mixture, see page 32
50 g/2 oz dried strawberries, chopped

TOPPING
5 tbsp strawberry jam
100 ml/3$^{1}/_{2}$ fl oz whipping cream
$^{1}/_{2}$ tsp pure vanilla extract
small fresh strawberries, halved, to decorate

# Strawberry and fresh cream cupcakes

1 Line an 8-hole muffin pan with large paper cases. Preheat the oven to 190°C/375°F/Gas 5.

2 Make up the Butterfly Cupcake mixture as directed in step 2 on page 32, then fold in the chopped, dried strawberries.

3 Spoon into the cake cases and bake for 22–25 minutes until risen and lightly golden, and just firm to the touch. Transfer to a wire rack to cool.

4 Using a teaspoon, carefully scoop out a circle about 2 cm/$^{3}/_{4}$ in deep from the top of each cake and reserve. Spoon a little strawberry jam into each of the cakes, then sit the reserved circle back on top.

5 Lightly whip the cream with the vanilla extract until just peaking. Transfer the cream to a piping bag fitted with a 1 cm/$^{1}/_{2}$ in star nozzle and pipe a swirl on top of each cake. Decorate with fresh strawberries and serve immediately.

classics 35

2

# indulgence

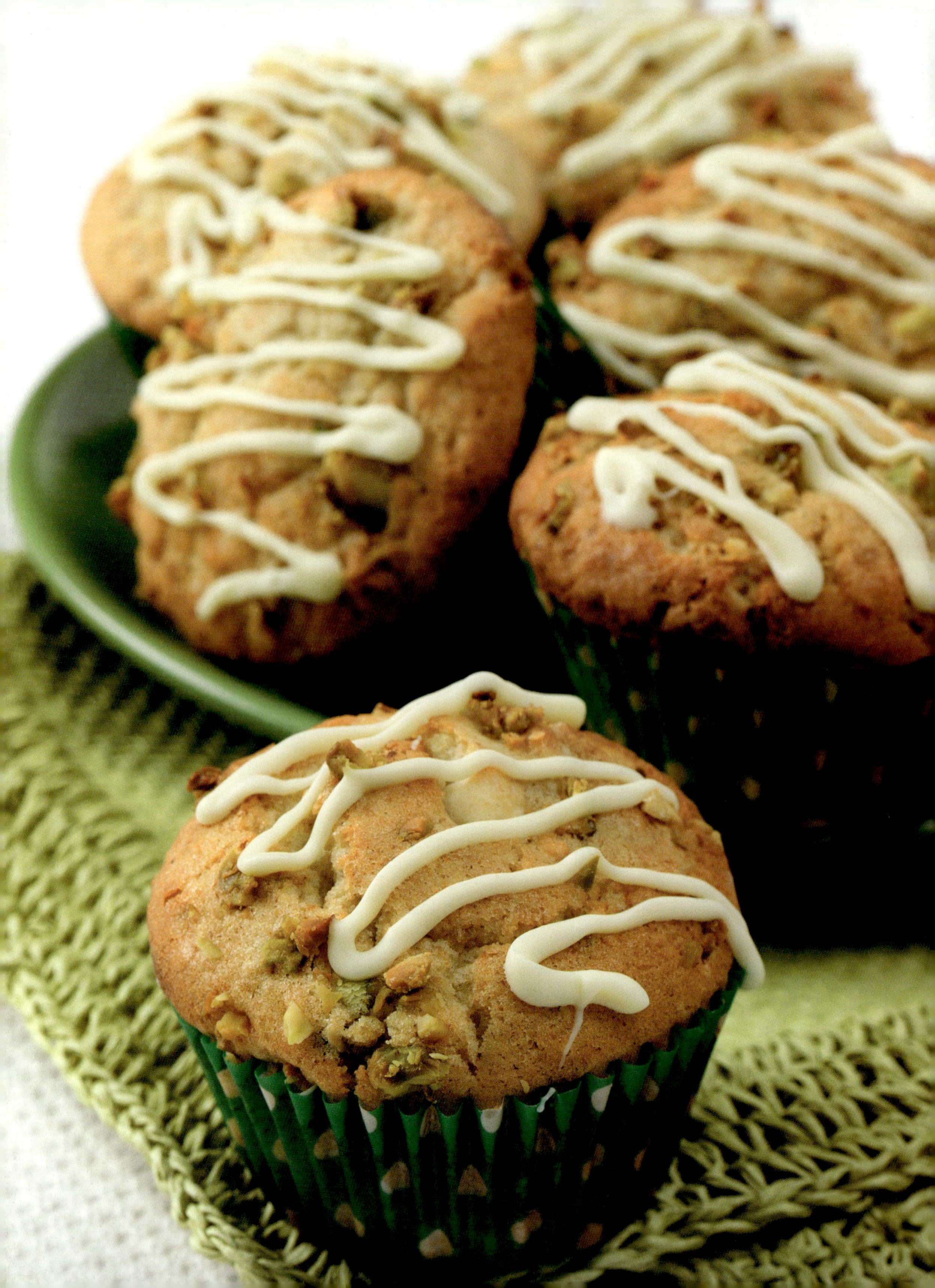

Makes 15
Prep time: 25 mins plus setting
Cook time: 23–25 mins

265 g/9 1/2 oz white chocolate chips
225 g/8 oz plain flour
1 tbsp baking powder
100 g/3 1/2 oz unsalted shelled pistachio nuts, ground

75 g/2 1/2 oz caster sugar
2 eggs, beaten
115 g/4 oz butter or margarine, melted
200 ml/7 fl oz whole milk
50 g/2 oz unsalted, shelled pistachios, lightly crushed

# White chocolate and pistachio muffins

1 Line a 15-hole muffin pan with large paper cases. Preheat the oven to 190°C/375°F/Gas 5.

2 Put 115 g/4 oz of the chocolate chips in a heatproof bowl and sit over a pan of barely simmering water until melted. Remove from the water and cool for 10 minutes.

3 Sift the flour and baking powder into a mixing bowl, then stir in the ground pistachios, sugar and all but 40 g/1 1/2 oz of the remaining chocolate chips. Make a well in the centre. In a measuring jug, mix together the eggs, melted butter or margarine and milk. Pour into the well and mix lightly to form a thick rough batter, then stir in the melted chocolate.

4 Spoon into the muffin cases, sprinkle each with crushed pistachios and bake for 23–25 minutes, until risen and golden. Transfer to a wire rack to cool.

5 Just before serving, melt the remaining chocolate chips as above and drizzle a little over each muffin. Stand for a few minutes to set before serving.

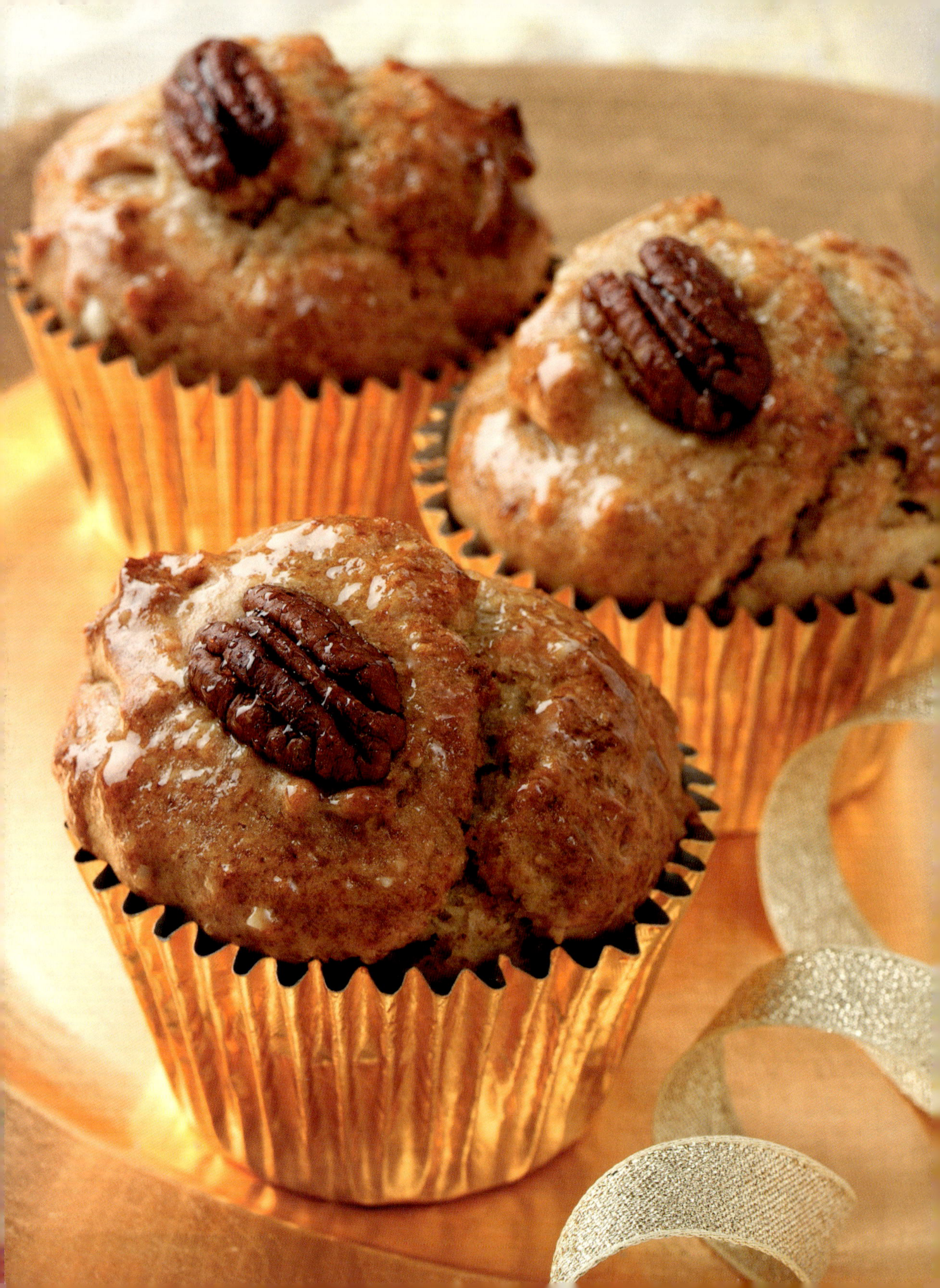

Makes 10
Prep time: 15 mins plus cooling
Cook time: 23–25 mins

350 g/12 oz plain flour
1 tsp bicarbonate of soda
115 g/4 oz pecan nuts, finely chopped

1 large egg, beaten
200 ml/7 fl oz buttermilk
125 ml/4$^{1}/_{2}$ fl oz maple syrup
100 ml/3$^{1}/_{2}$ fl oz sunflower oil
10 pecan halves

# Pecan and maple muffins

1 Line a 10-hole muffin pan with large paper cases. Preheat the oven to 190°C/375°F/Gas 5.

2 Sift the flour and bicarbonate of soda into a mixing bowl. Stir in the chopped pecans. Make a well in the centre.

3 In a measuring jug, mix together the egg, buttermilk, 100 ml/3$^{1}/_{2}$ fl oz of the maple syrup and the oil. Pour into the well and mix lightly to form a thick rough batter.

4 Spoon into the muffin cases, put a pecan half on top of each and bake for 23–25 minutes, until risen and lightly golden. Transfer to a wire rack and brush with remaining maple syrup to glaze. Best served warm.

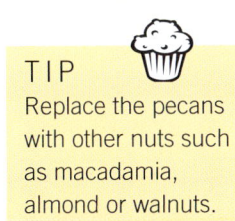

**TIP**
Replace the pecans with other nuts such as macadamia, almond or walnuts.

Makes 12
Prep time: 20 mins
Cook time: 16–18 mins

40 g/1½ oz plain chocolate-coated coffee beans
1 quantity Fairy Cupcake mixture, see page 27

TOPPING
150 ml/5 fl oz whipping cream
2 tsp drinking chocolate powder
12 small coffee bean-shaped chocolates (also called *chicchi di caffe*)

# Cappuccino cupcakes

1 Line a 12-hole cupcake pan with standard-size paper cases. Preheat the oven to 190°C/375°F/Gas 5.

2 Grind the chocolate-coated coffee beans in a coffee grinder or blender until fine and well ground.

3 Make up the Fairy Cupcake mixture as directed in steps 2 and 3 on page 27, then carefully stir in the ground coffee beans.

4 Spoon into the cake cases and bake for 16–18 minutes until lightly risen and just firm to the touch. Transfer to a wire rack to cool.

5 Lightly whip the cream until just peaking. Spoon on top of each cupcake to resemble the frothy milk on top of a cup of coffee. Dust lightly with drinking chocolate and decorate with a chocolate bean.

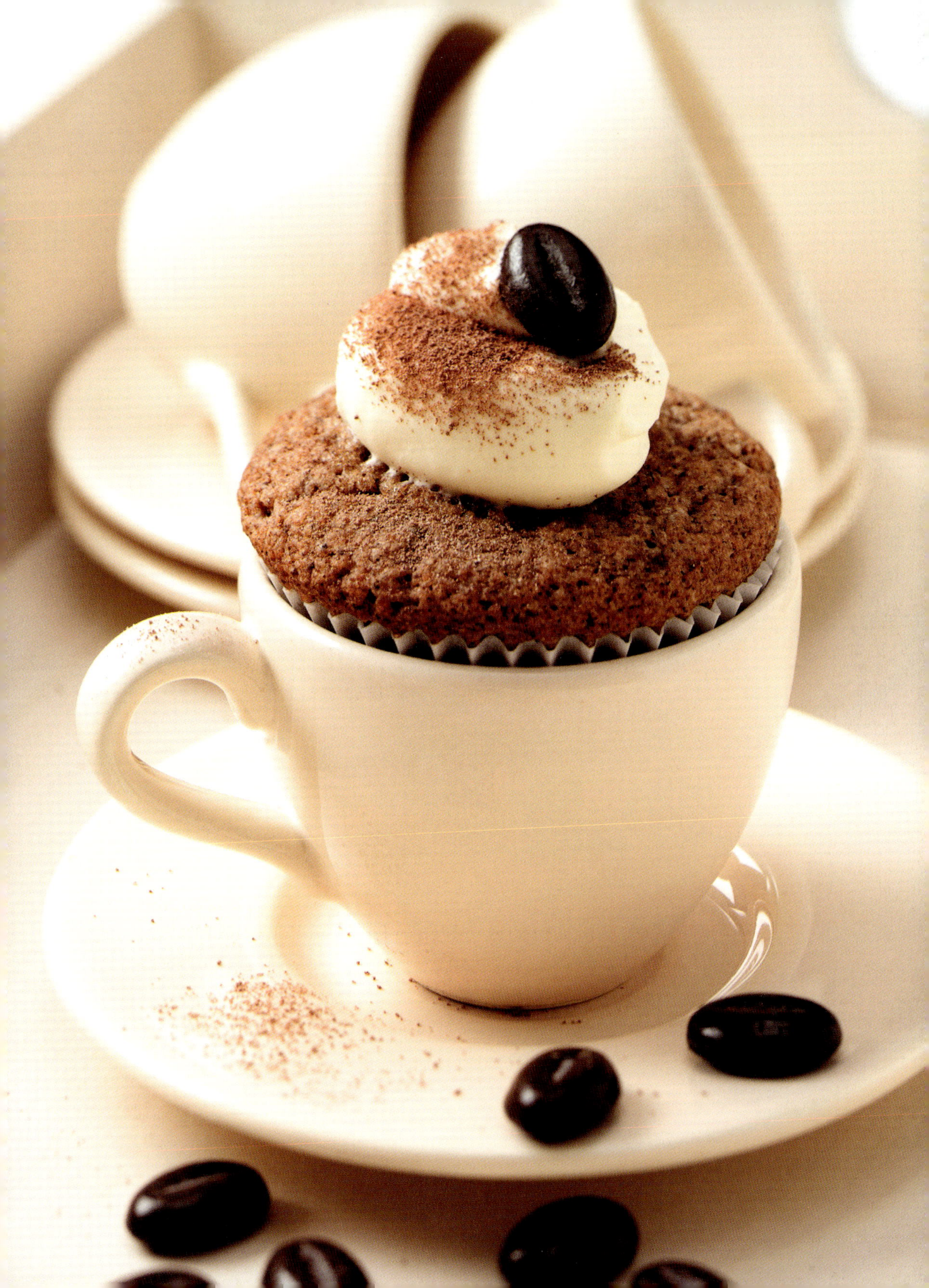

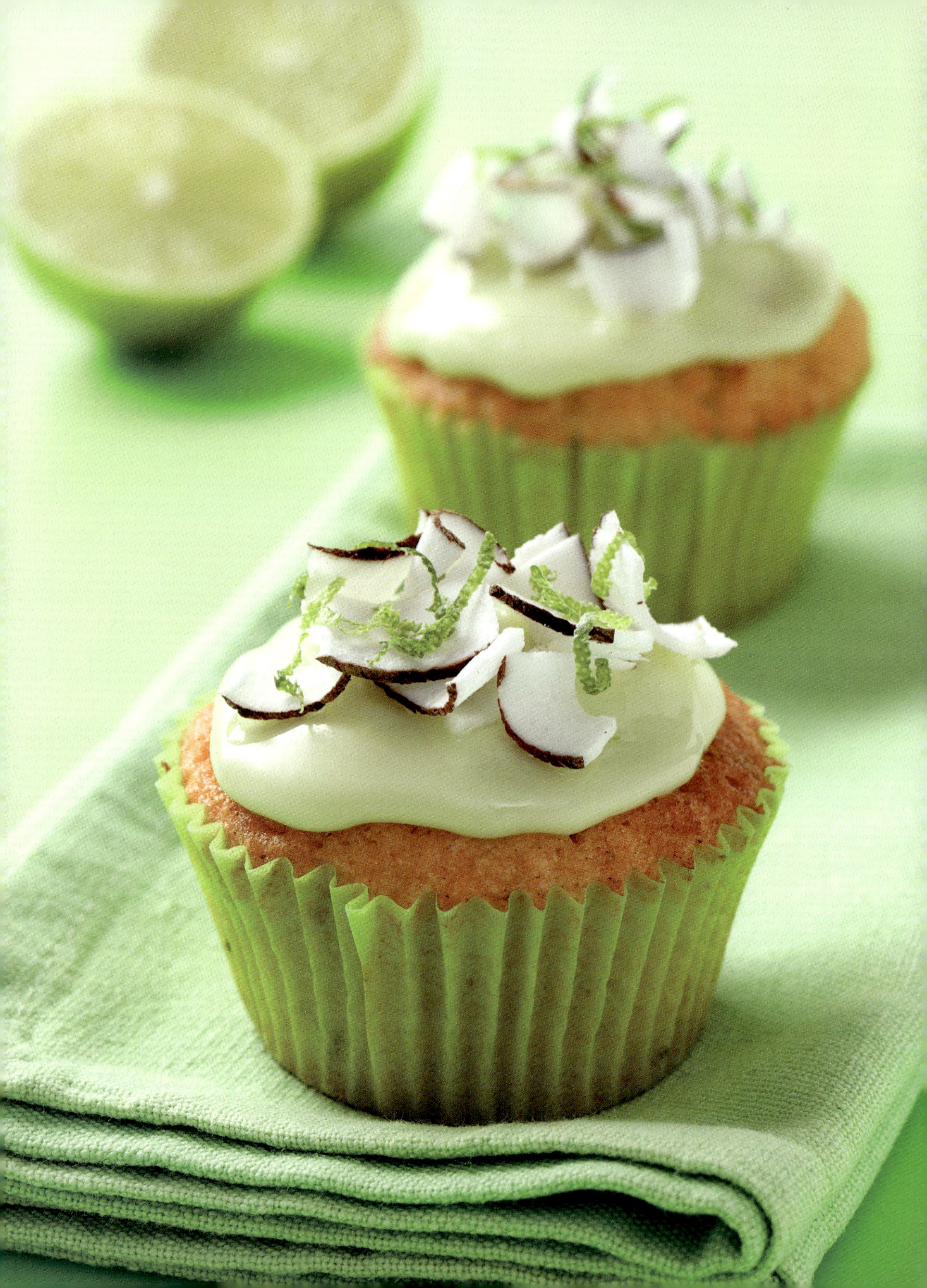

Makes 10
Prep time: 25 mins plus setting
Cook time: 16–18 mins

1 quantity plain Butterfly Cupcake mixture, see page 32 and below
50 g/2 oz finely grated fresh coconut
finely grated zest 1 lime

ICING
150 g/5 oz icing sugar
juice 1 lime
a few drops green food colouring (optional)
50 g/2 oz piece fresh coconut
lime zest, to decorate

# Fresh coconut and lime cupcakes

1 Line a 10-hole cupcake pan with standard-size paper cases. Preheat the oven to 190°C/375°F/Gas 5.

2 Make up the Butterfly Cupcake mixture as directed in step 2 on page 32 but omitting the vanilla extract, then carefully stir in the finely grated coconut together with the lime zest.

3 Spoon into the cake cases and bake for 16–18 minutes until risen and lightly golden, and just firm to the touch. Transfer to a wire rack to cool.

4 Sift the icing sugar into a bowl and gradually mix in sufficient lime juice to make a smooth, spreadable icing. Add a few drops of food colouring if liked.

5 Spread some of the lime icing over each cupcake. Using a vegetable peeler, shave off small pieces of coconut on top of each cake. Stand for a few minutes for the icing to set before serving decorated with lime zest.

TIP
For a more intense coconut flavour, use unsweetened desiccated coconut instead of fresh.

Makes 14
Prep time: 35 mins
Cook time: 25 mins

50 g/2 oz cocoa powder + extra to dust
115 g/4 oz butter, softened
275 g/9½ oz dark brown sugar, free of lumps

2 eggs, beaten
175 g/6 oz self-raising flour
¼ tsp baking powder

FROSTING
400 g/14 oz caster sugar
2 egg whites
¼ tsp cream of tartar
1 tsp pure vanilla extract

# Devil's food cupcakes

1 Line 14-hole muffin cake pans with large paper cases. Preheat the oven to 180°C/350°F/Gas 4.

2 Sift the cocoa powder into a bowl and gradually whisk in 225 ml/8 fl oz cold water. Set aside.

3 In a mixing bowl, beat the butter and sugar until well blended. Whisk in the eggs, then sift the flour and baking powder on top. Using a large metal spoon, carefully fold the flour into the batter along with the cocoa mixture.

4 Spoon into the cake cases to three-quarters fill them and bake for about 25 minutes until lightly risen and just firm to the touch. Transfer to a wire rack to cool.

5 For the frosting, put the sugar, egg whites and cream of tartar in a large heatproof bowl and whisk until thick. Place the bowl over a pan of barely simmering water and whisk until the sugar dissolves and the mix is thick and glossy.

6 Remove from the heat and whisk in the vanilla. Spoon into a piping bag fitted with a 5 mm/¼ in plain nozzle and pipe onto the cakes. Dust lightly with cocoa powder.

indulgence

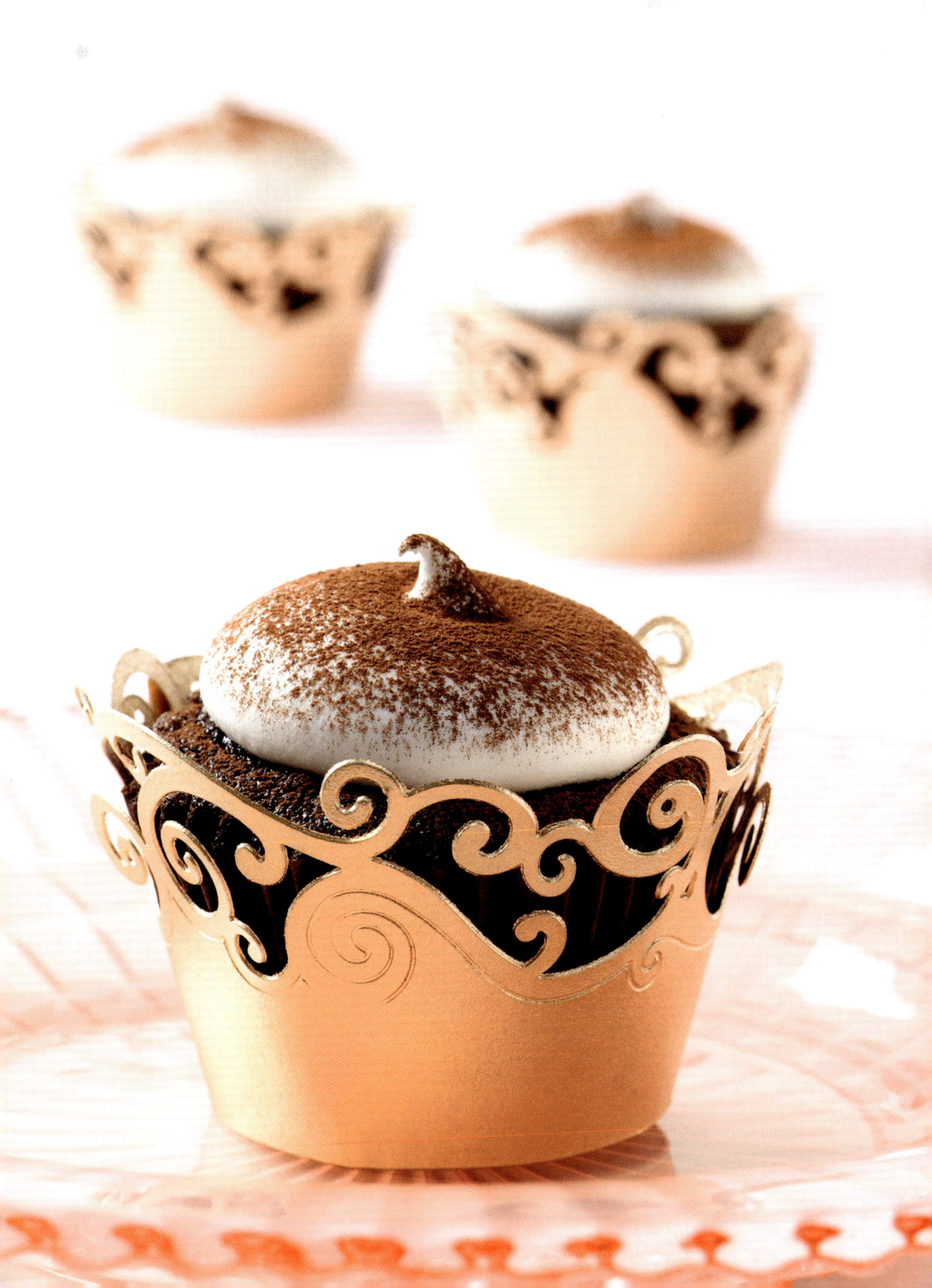

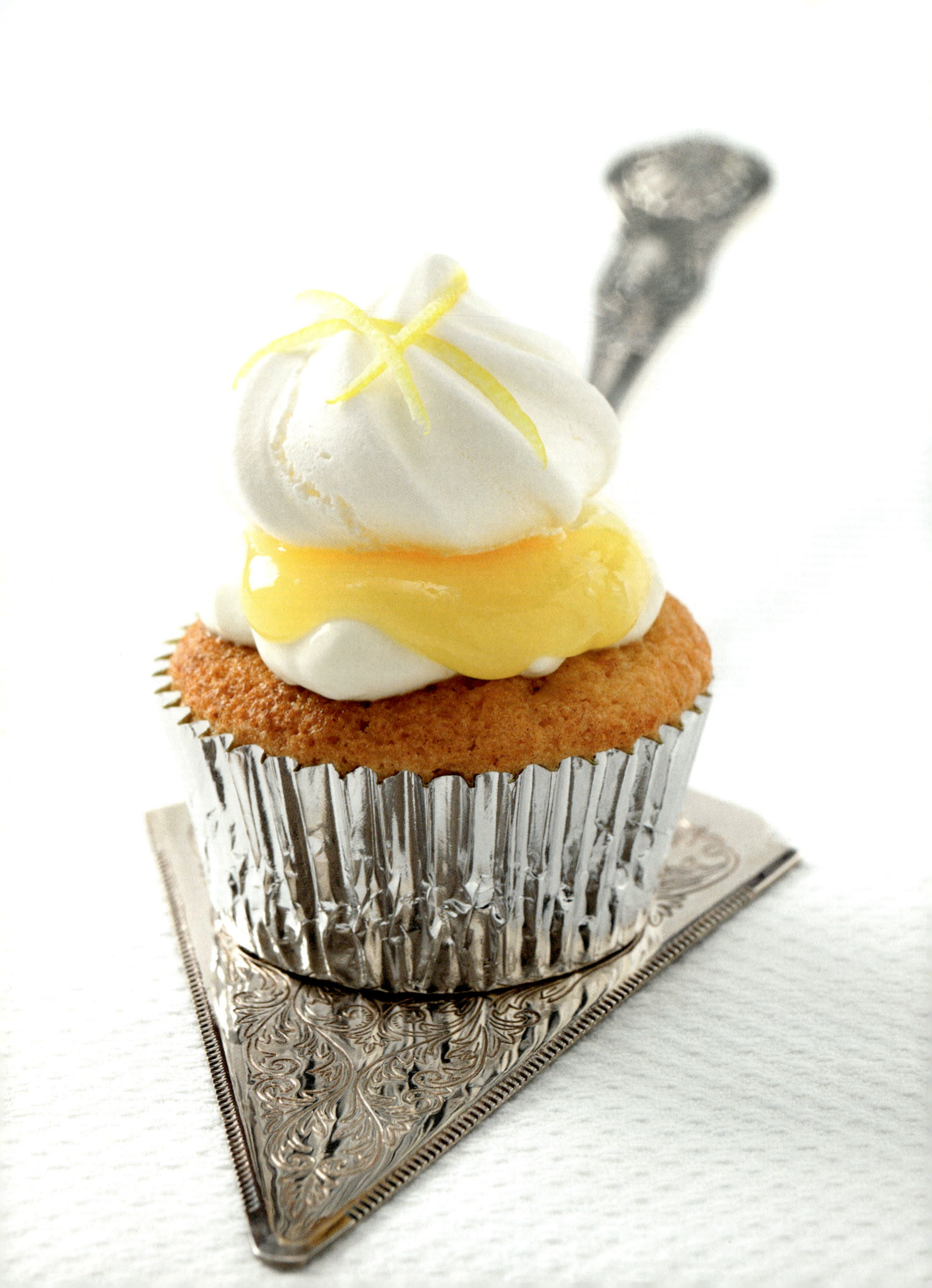

Makes 8
Prep time: 25 mins plus cooling
Cook time: 22–25 mins

1 quantity Fairy Cupcake mixture, see page 27
1 tsp finely grated lemon zest
150 g/5 oz good quality lemon curd

TOPPING
115 g/4 oz crème fraîche
8 mini meringues
strips of lemon zest

# Lemon meringue cupcakes

1 Line an 8-hole muffin pan with large paper cases. Preheat the oven to 190°C/375°F/Gas 5.

2 Make up the Fairy Cupcake mixture as directed in steps 2 and 3 on page 27, then carefully stir in the lemon zest.

3 Half-fill each cake case with the lemon cake mixture. Spoon a generous teaspoon of lemon curd on top, then cover with the remaining cake mixture. Bake for 22–25 minutes until risen and lightly golden, and just firm to the touch. Transfer to a wire rack to cool.

4 When ready to serve, spoon a generous dollop of crème fraîche on top of each cake, then some of the remaining lemon curd. Prop a mini meringue on top and decorate with lemon zest. Serve immediately.

indulgence

Makes 44
Prep time: 40 mins plus cooling
Cook time: 12–14 mins

115 g/4 oz 70% cocoa dark chocolate, broken into pieces
125 g/4½ oz butter
100 g/3½ oz caster sugar
2 eggs, beaten
50 g/2 oz self-raising flour
1 tsp baking powder
1 tsp ground cinnamon
1 tsp ground allspice
50 g/2 oz ground almonds
1 tsp finely grated orange zest

GANACHE-STYLE ICING

225 g/8 oz plain chocolate, broken into pieces
250 ml/9 fl oz double cream, at room temperature
edible gold leaf, to decorate

# Mini mayan gold cupcakes

1 Line 44-hole mini muffin pans with mini muffin paper cases. Preheat the oven to 180°C/350°F/Gas 4.

2 Put the chocolate and butter into a heatproof bowl and place over a saucepan of barely simmering water to melt. Remove from the water and stir in the sugar. Set aside for 10 minutes.

3 Gradually whisk the eggs into the chocolate mixture to make a thick, glossy batter. Sift the flour, baking powder and spices on top, then add the ground almonds and orange zest. Using a large metal spoon, carefully fold into the cake batter.

4 Spoon into the cake cases to almost fill them and bake for 12–14 minutes until lightly risen and just firm to the touch. Transfer to a wire rack to cool.

5 For the icing, melt the chocolate as above, then cool until only slightly warm. Whisk while slowly pouring in the cream. Continue whisking until glossy. Immediately, spoon into a piping bag fitted with a 1 cm/½ in star nozzle and pipe a swirl onto each cupcake. Just before serving, add a piece of gold leaf.

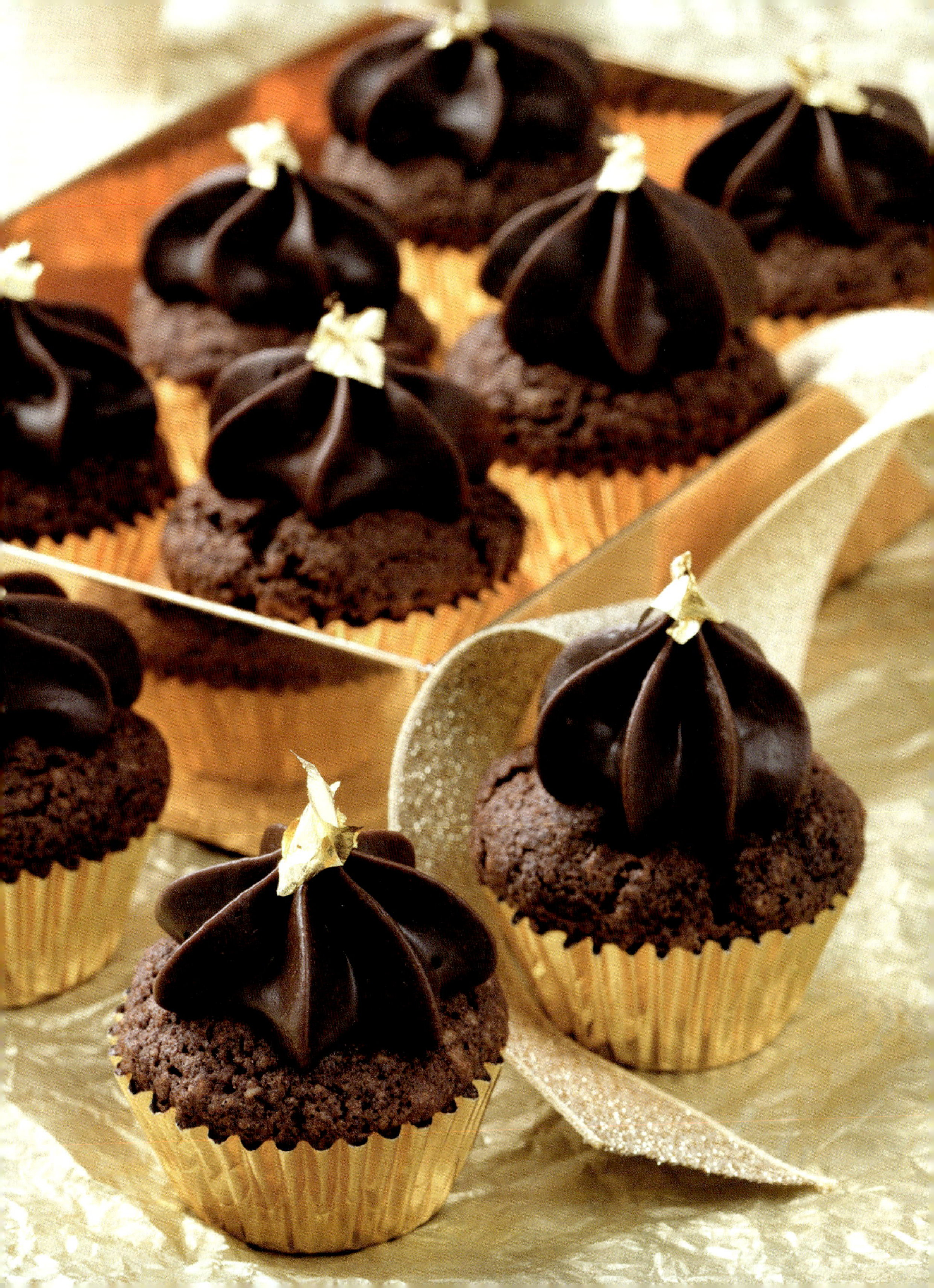

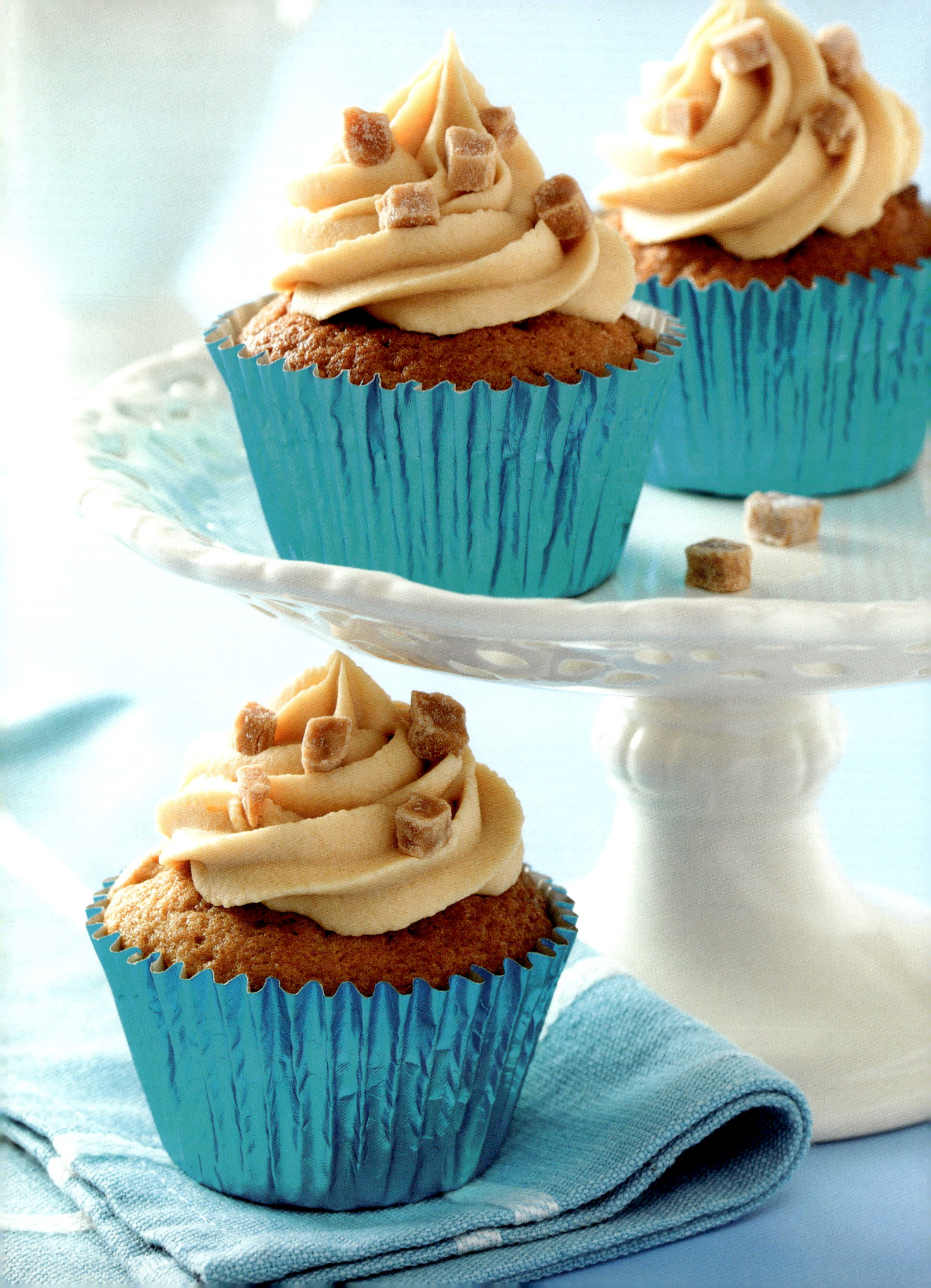

Makes 8
Prep time: 25 mins
Cook time: 22–25 mins

115 g/4 oz unsalted butter, softened
115 g/4 oz light brown sugar
1 tsp pure vanilla extract
2 eggs, beaten
115 g/4 oz plain flour

1½ tsp baking powder
100 g/3½ oz mini fudge pieces

ICING
75 g/3 oz unsalted butter, softened
150 g/5 oz icing sugar
4 tbsp caramel filling (also called *dulce de leche*)

# Sticky toffee cupcakes

1 Line an 8-hole muffin pan with large paper cases. Preheat the oven to 190°C/375°F/Gas 5.

2 In a mixing bowl, beat the butter with the sugar until pale, and creamy-light in texture. Stir in the vanilla extract.

3 Gradually whisk in the eggs, then sift the flour and baking powder on top. Add all but 25 g/1 oz of the fudge pieces, then, using a large metal spoon, carefully fold into the cake batter.

4 Spoon into the cake cases and bake for 22–25 minutes until lightly risen and lightly golden, and just firm to the touch. Transfer to a wire rack to cool.

5 For the icing, place the butter in a bowl and beat until soft. Gradually sift and beat in the icing sugar to make a smooth, creamy icing. Beat in the caramel filling.

6 Pile the icing into a piping bag fitted with a 1 cm/½ in star nozzle. Pipe a generous swirl on top of each cake and sprinkle with the remaining fudge pieces to serve.

indulgence

3

# wholesome

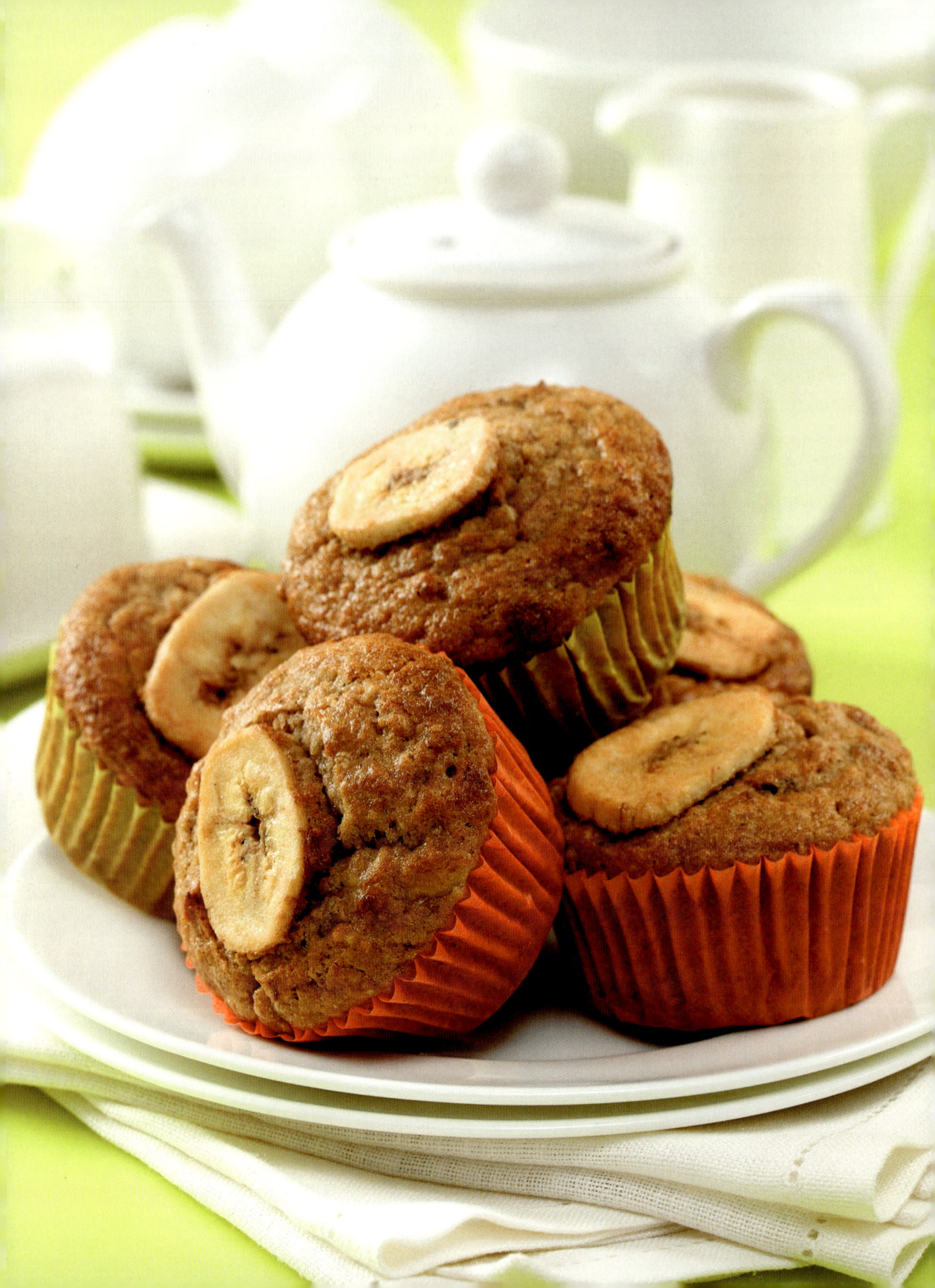

Makes 12
Prep time: 15 mins
Cook time: 22–25 mins

225 g/8 oz wholewheat plain flour
2 tsp baking powder
115 g/4 oz light brown sugar
115 g/4 oz breakfast muesli
1 egg, beaten
115 g/4 oz butter or margarine, melted
200 ml/7 fl oz whole milk
1 large ripe banana, peeled and mashed
1 tsp pure vanilla extract
12 dried banana chips

# Breakfast muesli and banana muffins

1 Line a 12-hole muffin pan with large paper cases. Preheat the oven to 190°C/375°F/Gas 5.

2 Sift the flour and baking powder into a mixing bowl, adding any husks that remain in the sieve. Stir in the sugar and muesli. Make a well in the centre.

3 In a measuring jug, mix together the egg, melted butter or margarine, milk, banana and vanilla extract. Pour into the well and mix lightly to form a thick rough batter.

4 Spoon into the muffin cases, put a banana chip on top of each and bake for 22–25 minutes, until risen and lightly golden. Transfer to a wire rack to cool. Best served warm.

Makes 12
Prep time: 15 mins
Cook time: 22–25 mins

50 g/2 oz + 2 tbsp porridge oats
225 g/8 oz wholewheat plain flour
2 tsp baking powder
200 g/7 oz prepared fresh blackberries

1 egg, beaten
115 g/4 oz butter or margarine, melted
150 ml/5 fl oz whole milk
115 g/4 oz strong-flavoured honey, such as heather

# Bramble, honey and oat muffins

1 Line a 12-hole muffin pan with large paper cases. Preheat the oven to 190°C/375°F/Gas 5.

2 Put 50 g/2 oz of the oats in a bowl and sift the flour and baking powder on top, adding any husks that remain in the sieve. Stir in the blackberries. Make a well in the centre.

3 In a measuring jug, mix together the egg, melted butter or margarine and milk. Pour into the well, add the honey and mix lightly to form a thick rough batter.

4 Spoon into the muffin cases and sprinkle each lightly with the remaining oats. Bake for 22–25 minutes, until risen and golden. Transfer to a wire rack to cool. Best served warm.

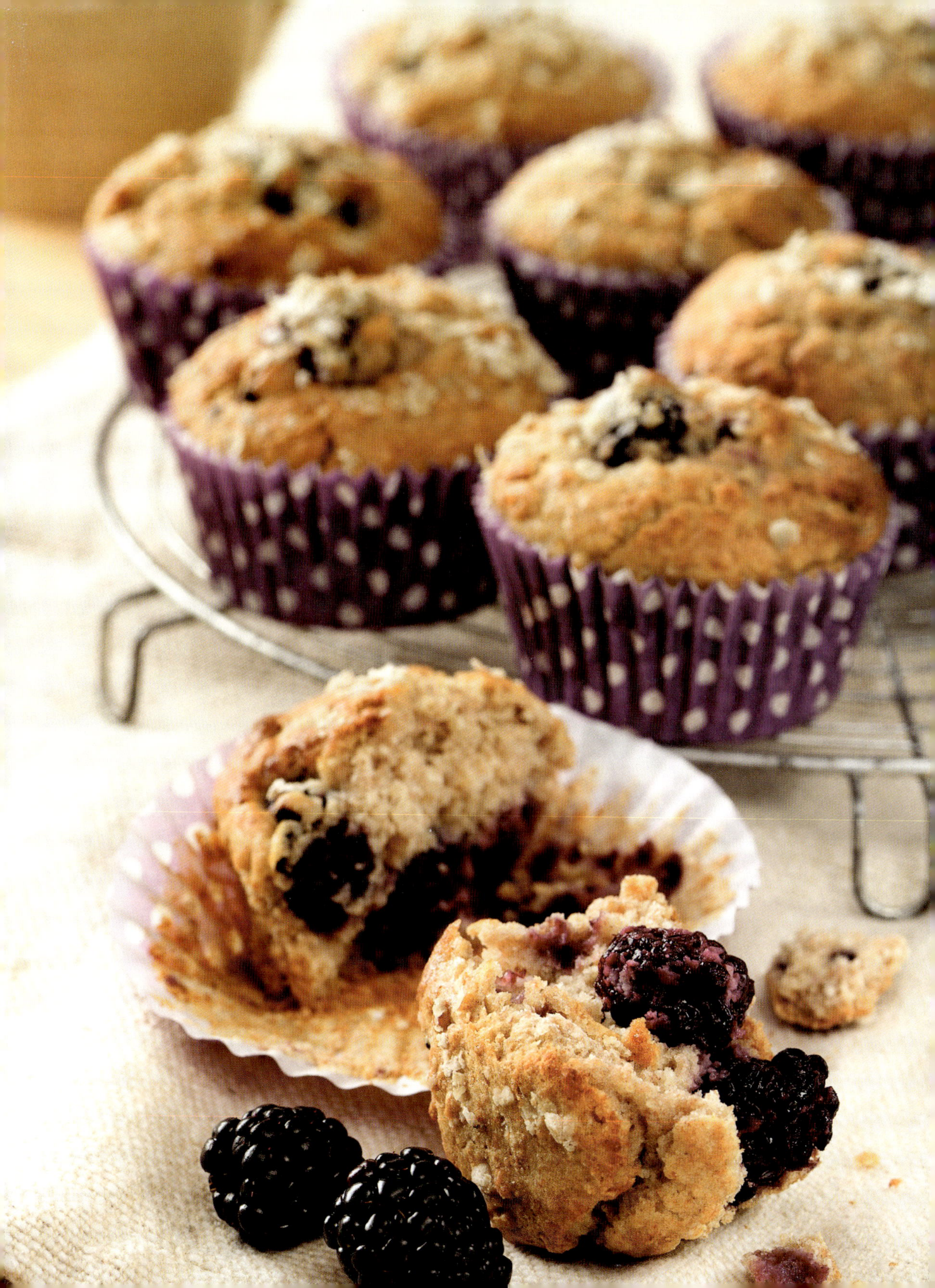

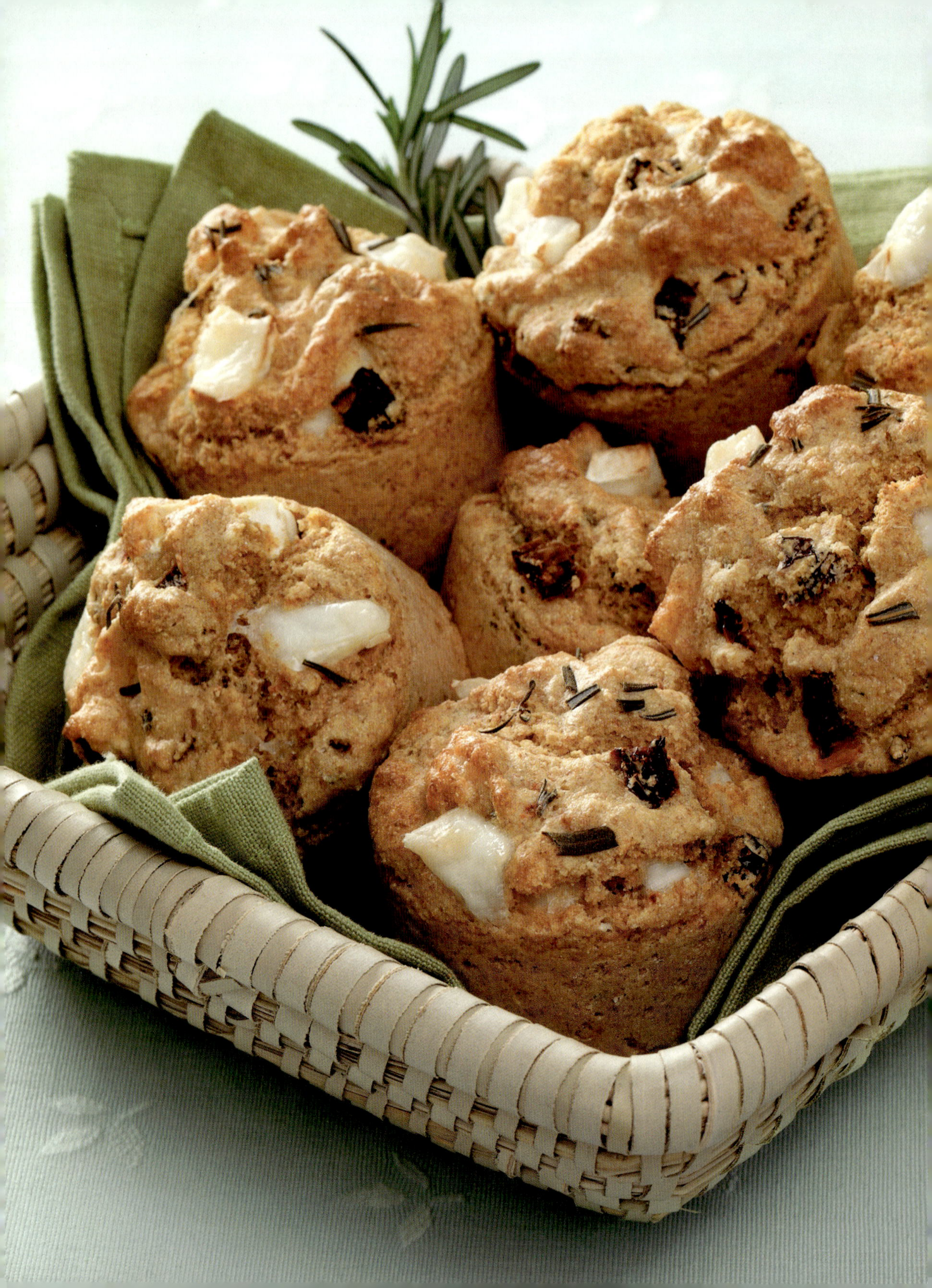

Makes 9
Prep time: 15 mins
Cook time: 20 mins

150 g/5 oz spelt or wholewheat flour
1 tbsp baking powder
salt and freshly ground black pepper
150 g/5 oz polenta or fine cornmeal
3 eggs, beaten
200 ml/7 fl oz whole milk
150 g/5 oz goats' cheese, crumbled or grated
50 g/2 oz dry pack sun-dried tomatoes, soaked and finely chopped
1 tbsp freshly chopped rosemary or 2 tsp dried
9 small sprigs fresh rosemary, to garnish
sweet tomato chutney, to serve

# Goat's cheese and tomato muffins

1 Grease a 9-hole muffin pan well or use a silicone muffin pan. Preheat the oven to 190°C/375°F/Gas 5.

2 Sift the flour, baking powder and seasoning into a bowl and add any wheat husks that remain in the sieve. Stir in the polenta and make a well in the centre.

3 Add the eggs and milk. Gradually mix together to form a smooth batter. Stir in the remaining ingredients except the garnish and chutney.

4 Spoon into the muffin pan and bake for about 20 minutes, until risen, golden and firm to the touch. Transfer to a wire rack to cool. Best served warm. Garnish with fresh rosemary and serve split and filled with sweet tomato chutney.

### TIP
Spelt flour is made from an ancient wheat grain *Triticum spelta*, used in Roman times. It is a light wholewheat flour with a lower gluten content than other wheat flours and makes a delicious soft-textured and wholesome cake mixture.

Makes 10
Prep time: 20 mins plus standing
Cook time: 25–30 mins

150 ml/5 fl oz cold pressed rapeseed oil or very light olive oil
150 g/5 oz unbleached caster sugar
2 eggs
125 g/4½ oz ground almonds
75 g/2½ oz semolina
finely grated zest 1 small orange
6 cardamom pods, green casings removed, seeds finely crushed
1 tsp baking powder
10 thin slices of small oranges

SYRUP
50 g/2 oz unbleached caster sugar
150 ml/5 fl oz freshly squeezed orange juice
a few drops orange flower water, to taste

# Orange and semolina muffins

1 Line a 10-hole muffin pan with large paper cases. Preheat the oven to 180°C/350°F/Gas 4.

2 Put the oil in a mixing bowl with the sugar and eggs and whisk together until well blended. Stir in the ground almonds and semolina until well mixed, then add the orange zest, cardamom and baking powder.

3 Spoon into the muffin cases, top with an orange slice and bake for 25–30 minutes, until risen and firm to the touch. Leave in the muffin pan.

4 Put the sugar and orange juice in a small saucepan and stir over a low heat until dissolved, then raise the heat and boil for 3–4 minutes until syrupy. Remove from the heat, cool slightly, then stir in orange flower water to taste.

5 Prick the hot muffins with a fork and spoon a little syrup over each. Stand for 30 minutes before serving.

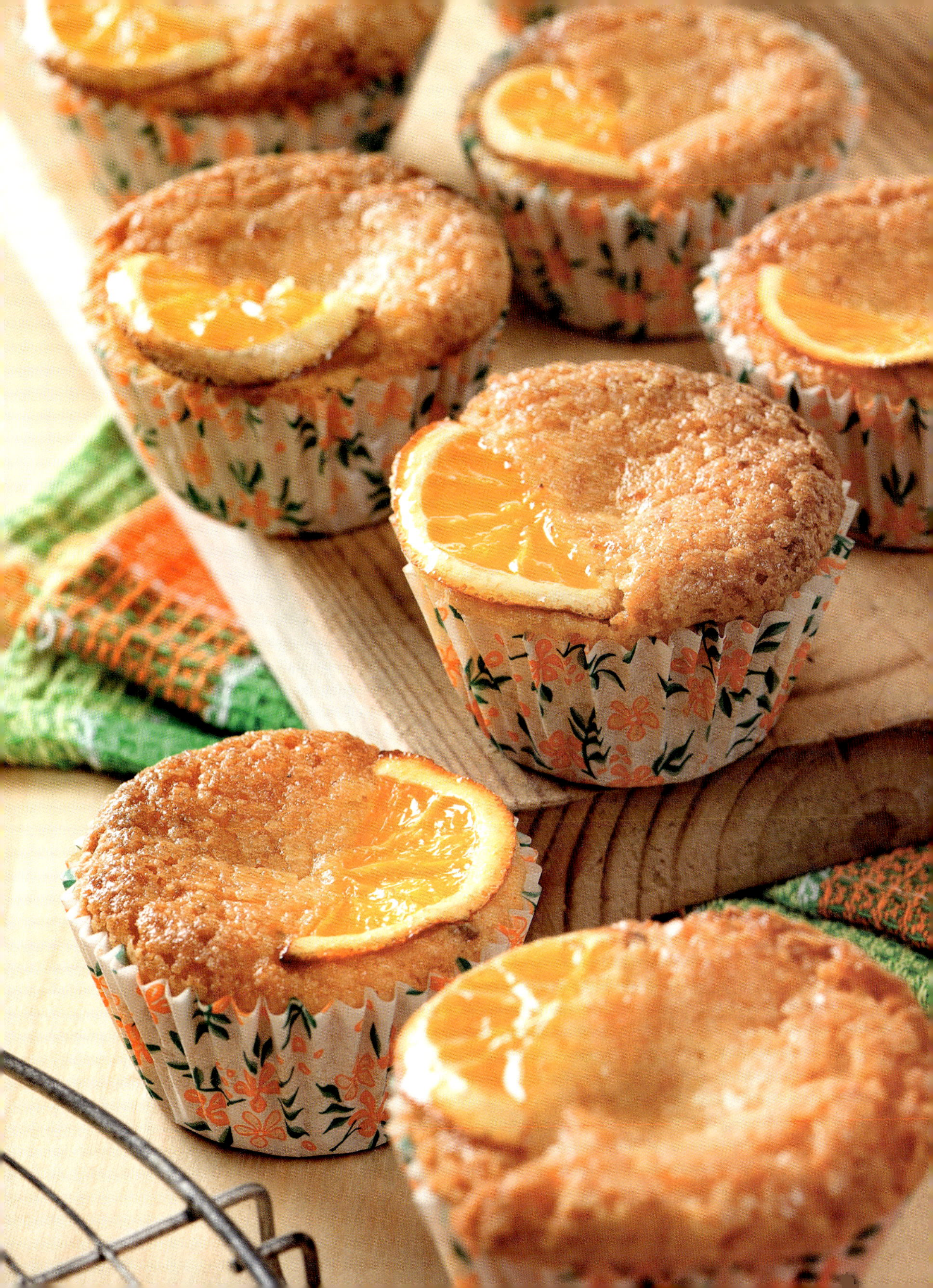

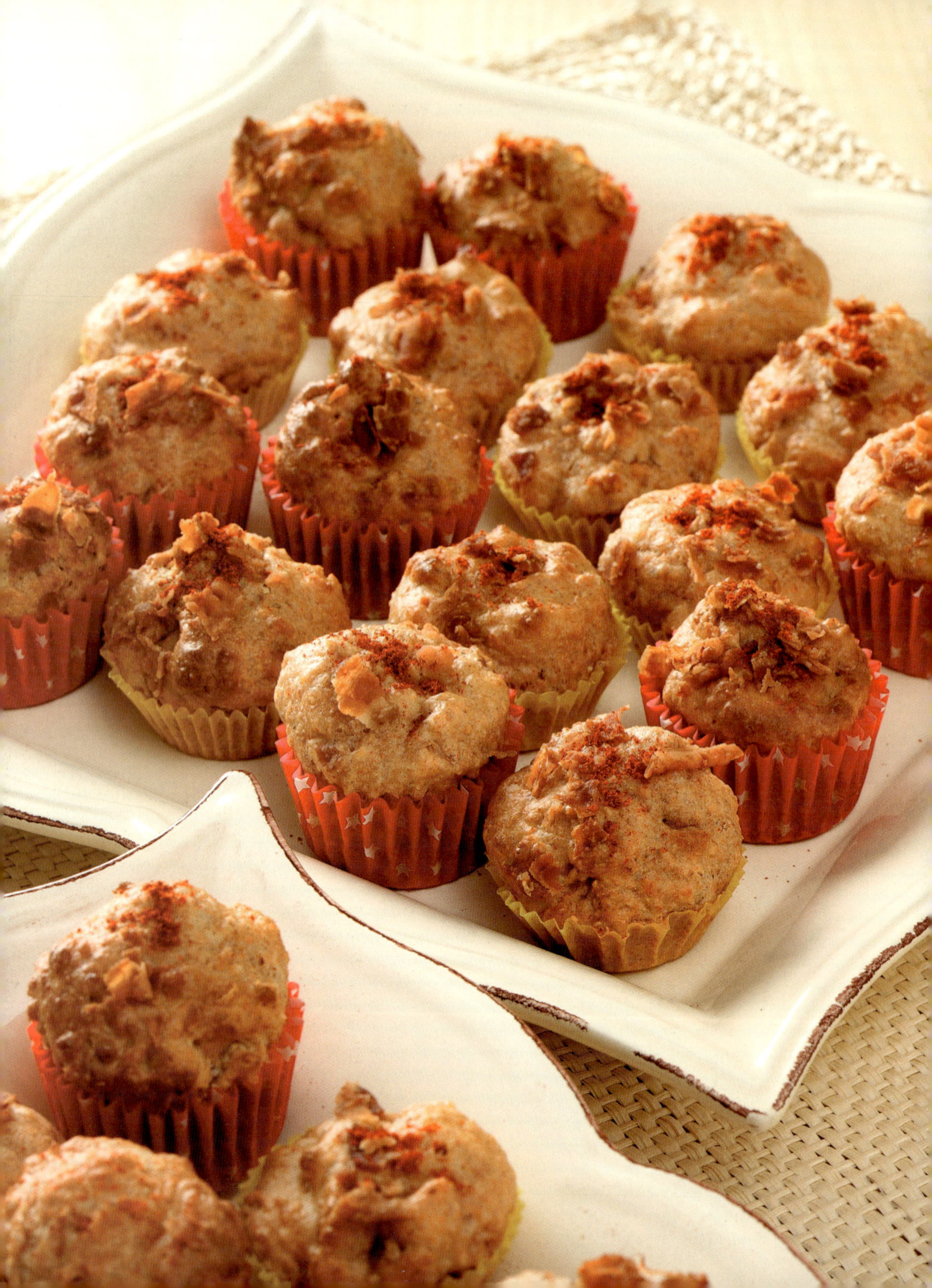

Makes 30
Prep time: 20 mins
Cook time: 12 mins

225 g/8 oz spelt or wholewheat flour
2 tsp baking powder
1 tsp smoked paprika + extra to dust
salt and freshly ground black pepper
75 g/2½ oz cooked smoked bacon, finely chopped
75 g/2½ oz freshly grated Parmesan cheese
2 eggs, beaten
200 ml/7 fl oz whole milk

# Smoky bite-sized cheese and bacon muffins

1 Line 30-hole mini muffin pans with mini muffin paper cases. Preheat the oven to 200°C/400°F/Gas 6.

2 Sift the flour, baking powder, smoked paprika and seasoning into a bowl and add any wheat husks that remain in the sieve. Stir in the bacon and cheese. Make a well in the centre.

3 Add the eggs and milk. Gradually mix together to form a smooth batter.

4 Spoon the mixture into the muffin cases to fill them and bake for about 12 minutes, until risen, and just firm to the touch. Transfer to a wire rack to cool. Best served warm, dusted with extra paprika.

### TIP
Smoked paprika adds a delicious sweet-smoke flavour to baking; varieties can be mild or hot. Use plain sweet paprika or regular chilli powder if preferred.

wholesome

Makes 9
Prep time: 25 mins
Cook time: 20 mins

115 g/4 oz plain flour
2 tsp baking powder
1/2 tsp bicarbonate of soda
150 g/5 oz yellow cornmeal or polenta
3 tbsp caster sugar
1 egg, beaten

225 ml/8 fl oz buttermilk
50 g/2 oz butter or margarine, melted
2 spring onions, trimmed and finely chopped
50 g/2 oz cooked red pepper, finely chopped
50 g/2 oz cooked sweetcorn kernels
salt and freshly ground black pepper
1–2 tsp dried chilli flakes, to taste
9 slices jalapeño pepper

# Mexican cornbread muffins

1 Line a 9-hole muffin pan with large paper cases. Preheat the oven to 190°C/375°F/Gas 5.

2 Sift the flour, baking powder and bicarbonate of soda into a mixing bowl and stir in the cornmeal and sugar. Make a well in the centre.

3 Add the egg, buttermilk and melted butter or margarine Gently mix together to form a smooth batter. Stir in the onions, peppers, sweetcorn, seasoning and chilli flakes to taste.

4 Spoon into the muffin cases and place a slice of jalapeño on top of each. Bake for about 20 minutes, until risen, golden and firm to the touch. Transfer to a wire rack to cool. Best served warm.

**TIP**
Use cornmeal if you can, as it is often more finely ground than polenta.

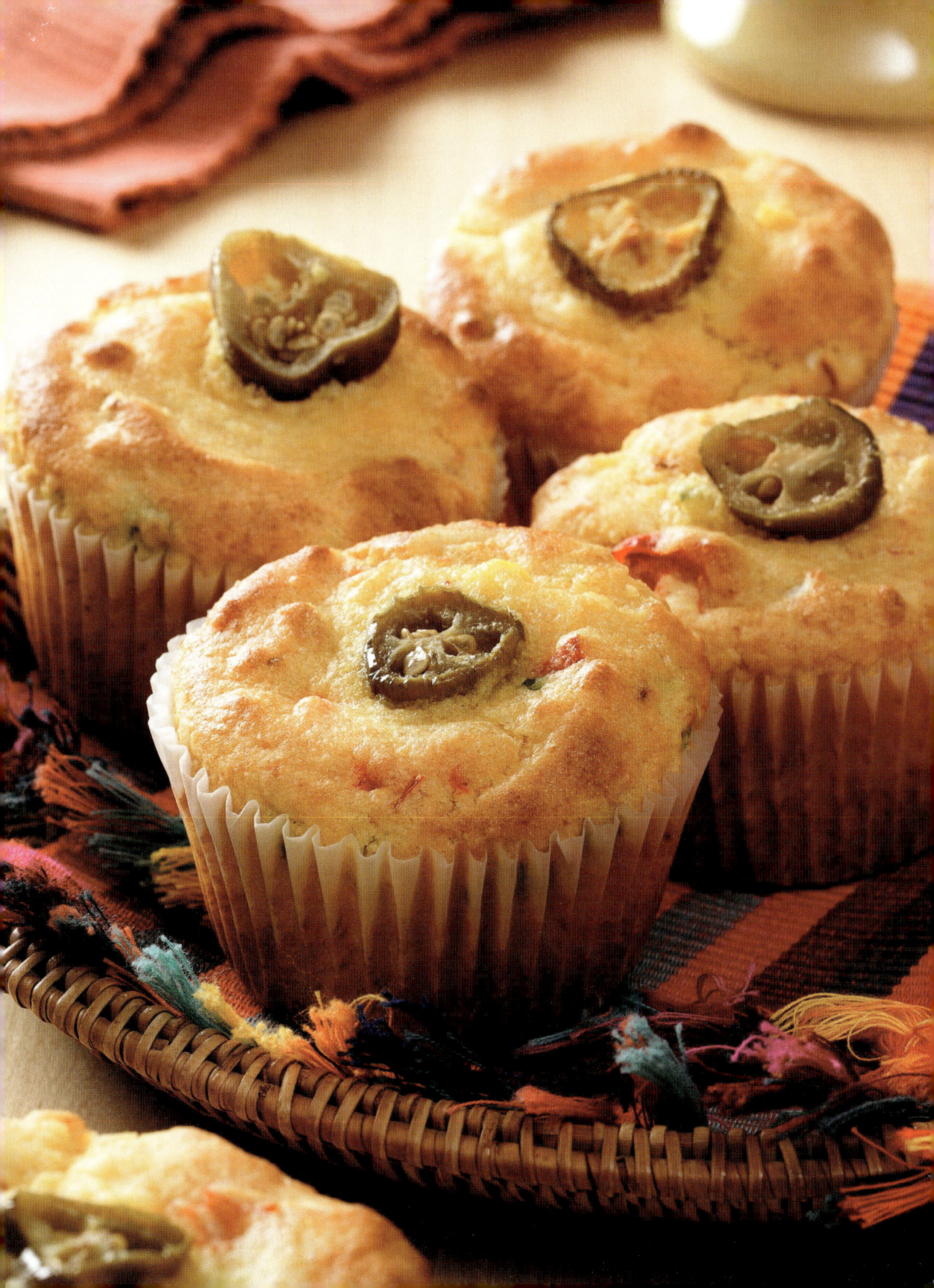

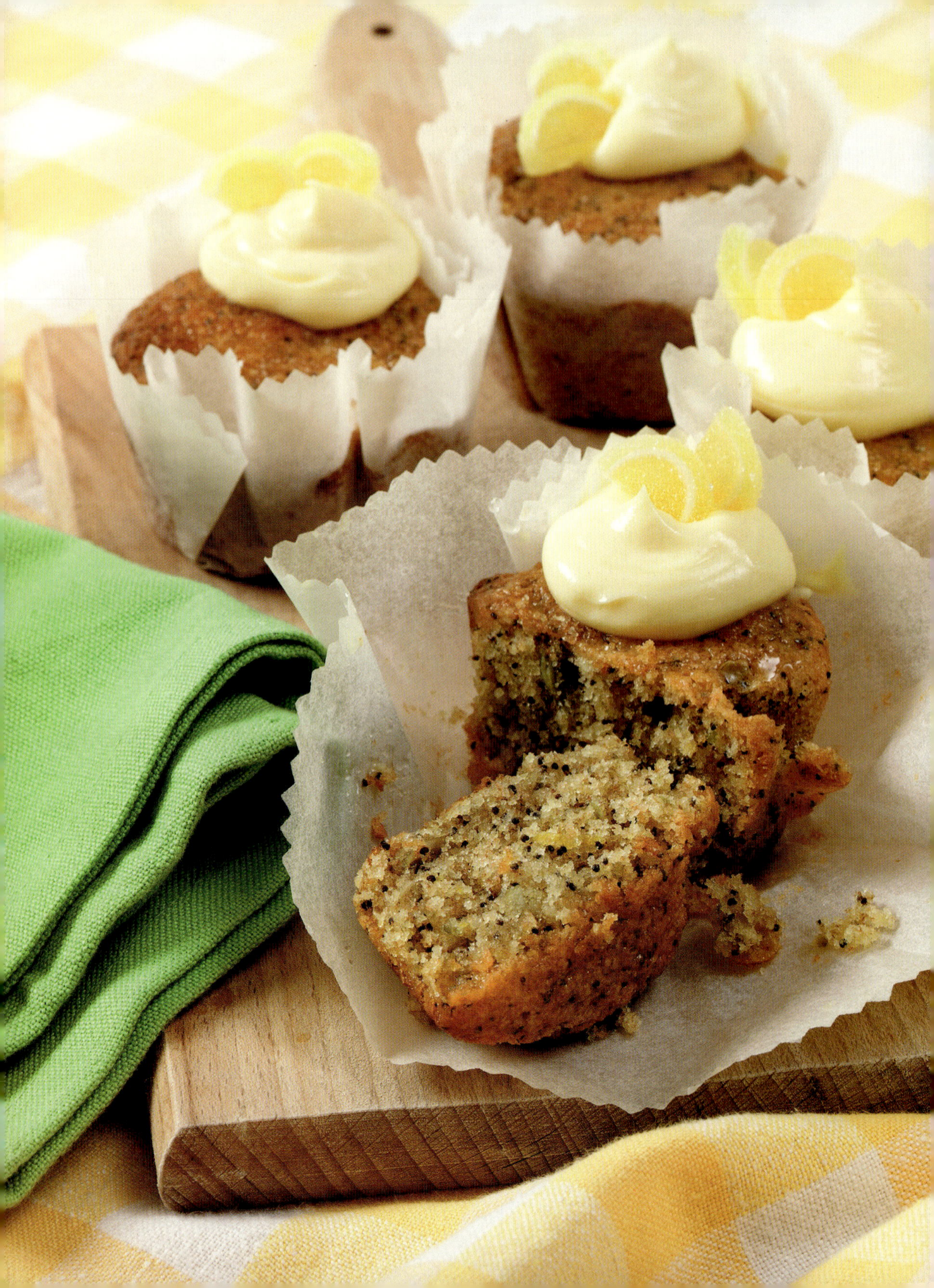

Makes 9
Prep time: 20 mins
Cook time: 18–20 mins

115 g/4 oz butter or vegetable margarine, softened
115 g/4 oz caster sugar
finely grated zest 1 lemon
2 eggs, beaten
75 g/2½ oz spelt flour
1 tsp baking powder

50 g/2 oz ground almonds
2 tbsp poppy seeds
25 g/1oz pumpkin seeds, chopped

SYRUP AND TOPPING
50 g/2 oz caster sugar
juice 1 lemon made up to 150 ml/5 fl oz with cold water
200 g/7 oz soft cheese
4 tbsp good quality lemon curd
lemon jelly slices, to decorate

# Seeded lemon cupcakes

1 Line a 9-hole cupcake pan with home-made (see page 12) or tulip baking cases. Preheat the oven to 190°C/375°F/Gas 5.

2 In a mixing bowl, beat the butter or margarine with the sugar until pale and creamy. Stir in the lemon zest. Gradually whisk in the eggs, then sift the flour and baking powder on top, adding any husks that remain in the sieve. Add the ground almonds and seeds, then fold into the batter.

3 Spoon into the cake cases and bake for 18–20 minutes until slightly risen, lightly golden and just firm to the touch. Leave in the cake pan.

4 To make the syrup. Put the sugar and diluted lemon juice in a small saucepan. Stir over a low heat until dissolved, then raise the heat and boil for 3–4 minutes until syrupy. Prick the hot cupcakes with a fork and spoon a little syrup over each. Stand for 10 minutes before transferring to a wire rack to cool.

5 To serve, mix the soft cheese and lemon curd together and spoon on top of each cupcake. Decorate with lemon jelly slices.

wholesome

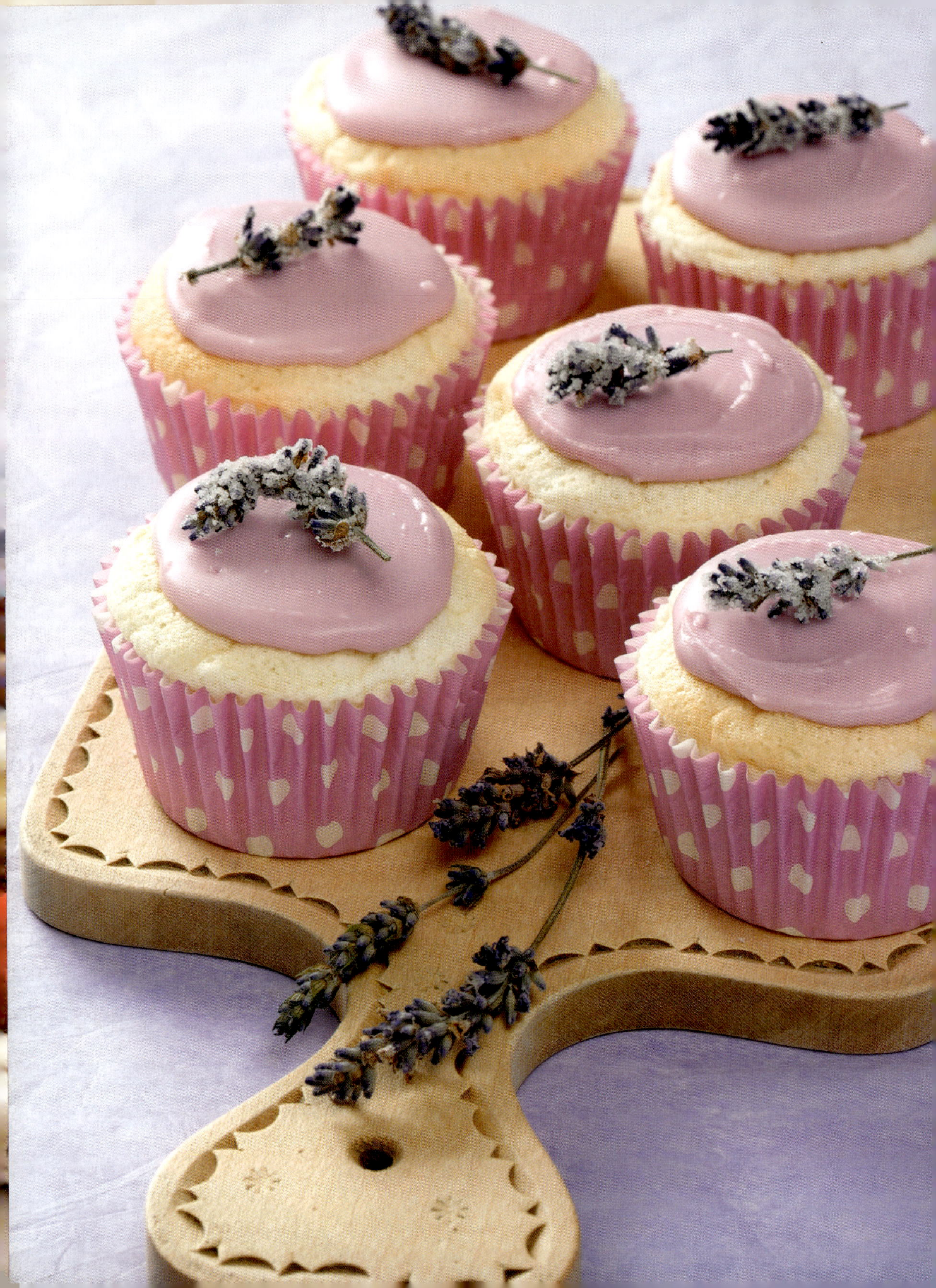

Makes 8
Prep time: 25 mins plus setting
Cook time: 10–12 mins

50 g/2 oz plain flour
75 g/2½ oz caster sugar
3 large egg whites
½ tsp cream of tartar
½ tsp pure vanilla extract

ICING
150 g/5 oz icing sugar
pinch dried lavender, finely ground
lilac food colouring
sugared lavender flowers, to decorate

# Angelic lavender cupcakes

1 Line an 8-hole muffin pan with large paper cases. Preheat the oven to 180°C/350°F/Gas 4.

2 Sift the flour and half the caster sugar into a small bowl.

3 In a large, grease-free bowl, whisk the egg whites until softly peaking but not stiff. Add the cream of tartar, remaining sugar and the vanilla extract. Continue whisking until thick and glossy. Sift in the flour and sugar mix, folding in gently after each addition until well combined.

4 Spoon the mixture into the cake cases to fill them and bake for 10–12 minutes until very lightly golden and slightly springy to the touch. Transfer to a wire rack to cool.

5 To ice, sift the icing sugar into a bowl. Add the ground lavender and gradually mix in sufficient warm water to make a smooth icing. Mix in a few drops of food colouring.

**TIP**
To make the flowers, lightly brush small dried flowerheads of lavender with lightly beaten egg white, then dip in caster sugar. Leave to dry on a sheet of baking parchment.

6 Spread the icing over each cake and decorate with lavender flowers. Allow to set.

wholesome

4

# celebrations

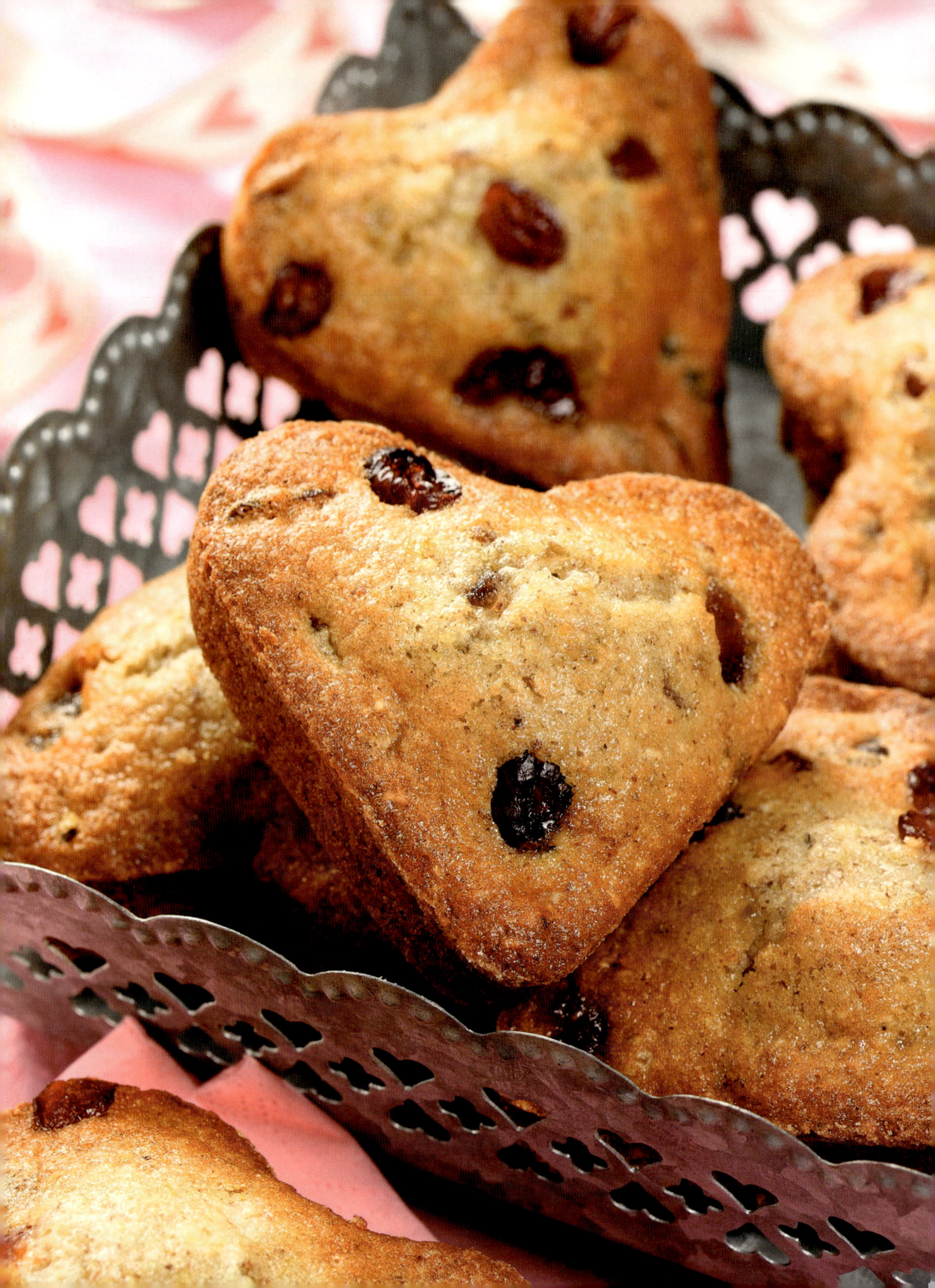

Makes 10
Prep time: 10 mins
Cook time: 15–16 mins

115 g/4 oz plain flour
2 tsp baking powder
115 g/4 oz ground hazelnuts
115 g/4 oz caster sugar

175 g/6 oz assorted dried red berry fruits, such as cranberries, strawberries, cherries
1 egg, beaten
50 g/2 oz butter or margarine, melted
175 ml/6 fl oz whole milk
1 tsp pure vanilla extract

# Partnership muffins

1 Grease a 10-hole heart-shaped muffin pan or use heart-shaped silicone muffin moulds. Preheat the oven to 190°C/375°F/Gas 5.

2 Sift the flour and baking powder into a mixing bowl, then stir in the ground hazelnuts, sugar and red berries. Make a well in the centre.

3 In a measuring jug, mix together the egg, melted butter or margarine, milk and vanilla extract. Pour into the well and mix lightly to form a rough batter.

4 Spoon into the muffin pan and bake for 15–16 minutes, until risen and golden. Transfer to a wire rack to cool a little. These are best served warm.

Makes 8
Prep time: 15 mins
Cook time: 22–25 mins

225 g/8 oz plain flour
2 tsp baking powder
2 tsp mixed spice
115 g/4 oz light brown sugar
175 g/6 oz luxury dried fruit mix

1 egg, beaten
50 g/2 oz butter or margarine, melted
175 ml/6 fl oz whole milk

TOPPING
icing sugar, to dust
175 g/6 oz piece golden marzipan
2 tbsp apricot jam, sieved

# Hot cross bun muffins

**1** Line an 8-hole muffin pan with large paper cases. Preheat the oven to 190°C/375°F/Gas 5.

**2** Sift the flour, baking powder and spice into a mixing bowl, then stir in the sugar and dried fruit. Make a well in the centre.

**3** In a measuring jug, mix together the egg, melted butter or margarine and milk. Pour into the well and mix lightly to form a rough batter.

**4** Spoon into the muffin cases and bake for 22–25 minutes, until risen and golden. Transfer to a wire rack to cool. Best served warm.

**5** To finish, lightly dust the work surface with icing sugar and roll out the marzipan thinly to form a rectangle 20 x 10 cm/8 x 4 in. Cut into 16 thin strips. Brush the tops of the muffins with a little jam and secure a marzipan cross on top.

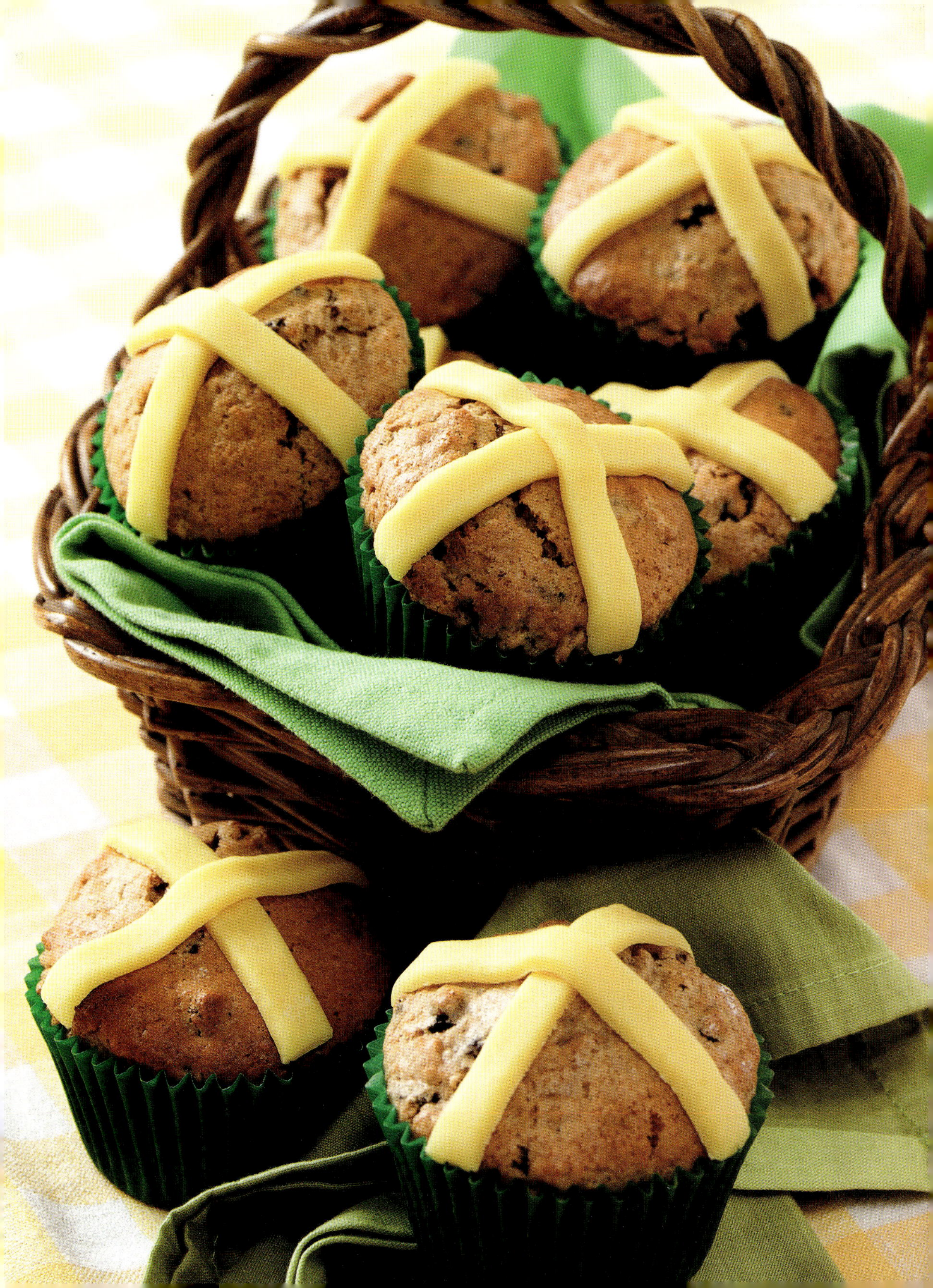

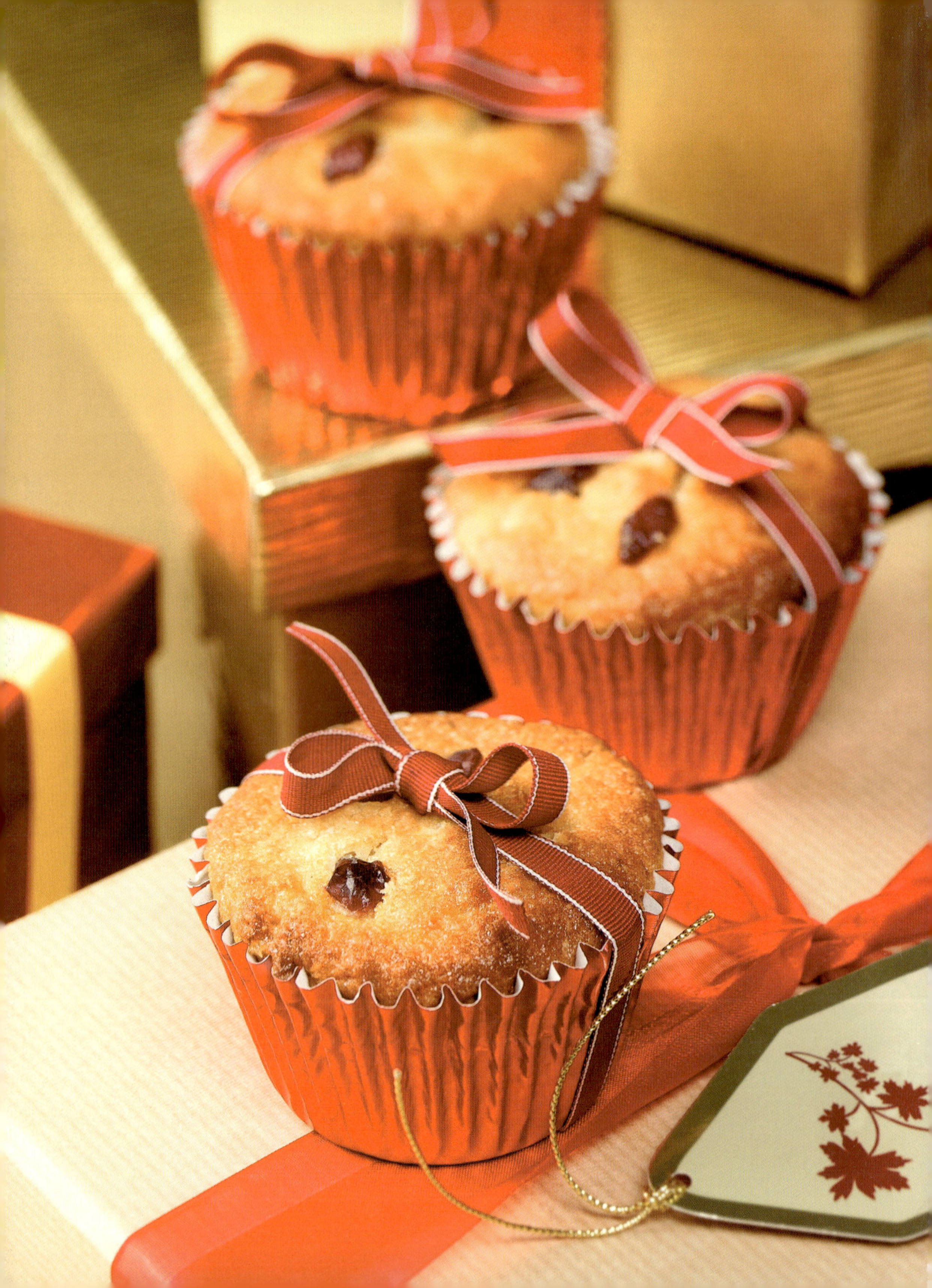

Makes 9
Prep time: 15 mins
Cook time: 22–25 mins

115 g/4 oz plain flour
2 tsp baking powder
115 g/4 oz ground almonds
115 g/4 oz light brown sugar
115 g/4 oz dried cranberries
115 g/4 oz golden marzipan, cut into small pieces
1 egg, beaten
50 g/2 oz butter or margarine, melted
175 ml/6 fl oz whole milk
9 short lengths of festive ribbon, to decorate

# Festive cranberry and marzipan muffins

1 Line a 9-hole muffin pan with large paper cases. Preheat the oven to 190°C/375°F/Gas 5.

2 Sift the flour and baking powder into a mixing bowl, then stir in the ground almonds, sugar, cranberries and chopped marzipan. Make a well in the centre.

3 In a measuring jug, mix together the egg, melted butter or margarine and milk. Pour into the well and mix lightly to form a thick rough batter.

4 Spoon into the muffin cases and bake for 22–25 minutes, until risen and golden. Transfer to a wire rack to cool a little. Best served warm. Tie with festive ribbon before serving.

Makes 12
Prep time: 35 mins plus setting
Cook time: 16–18 mins

1 quantity Chocolate Fairy Cupcake mixture, see page 27
4 tbsp good quality chocolate spread

TOPPING
175 g/6 oz milk chocolate, broken into pieces
white and yellow mini marshmallows
50 g/2 oz chocolate fondant icing
50 g/2 oz yellow fondant icing
assorted tubes of ready-made, coloured writing icing

# Easter animal cupcakes

1 Line a 12-hole cupcake pan with standard-size paper cases. Preheat the oven to 190°C/375°F/Gas 5.

2 Make up the Chocolate Fairy Cupcake mixture as directed in steps 2 and 3 and the tip on page 27.

3 Half-fill each cupcake case with the mixture. Spoon 1 teaspoon of the chocolate spread on top and cover with the remaining cake mixture. Bake for 16–18 minutes until risen, lightly golden and just firm to the touch. Transfer to a wire rack to cool.

4 To ice, put the chocolate in a heatproof bowl and place over a saucepan of gently simmering water to melt. Remove the saucepan from the heat.

5 Working on one cupcake at a time, spread the top with melted chocolate, then arrange marshmallows on top before the chocolate sets. Keep the melted chocolate sitting on the warm water to help prevent it from setting.

6 Once the marshmallows have set in place, roll out the 2 pieces of fondant separately and cut to make faces and ears for the sheep and faces for the chicks. Pipe features on top of each and place over the marshmallows.

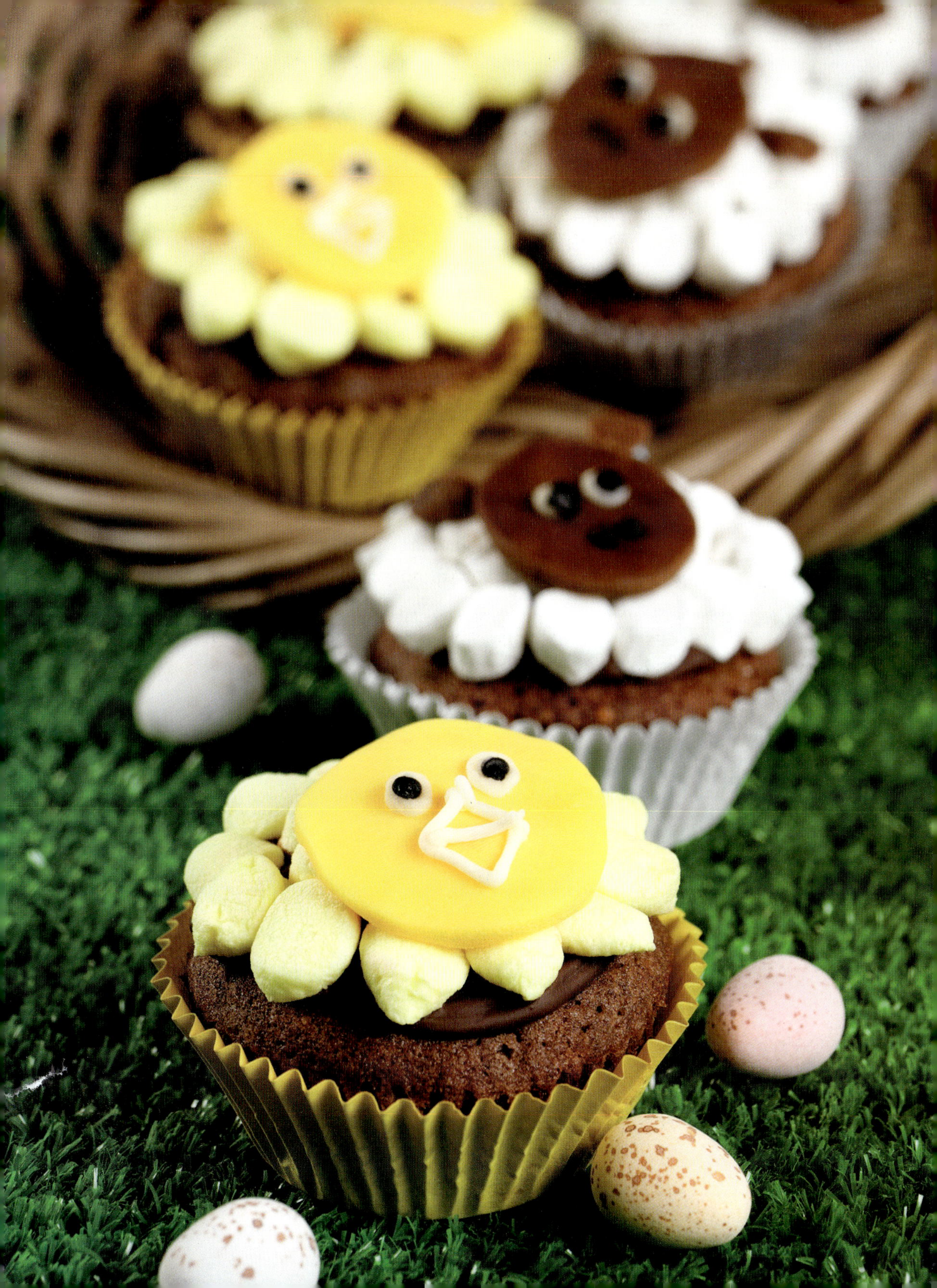

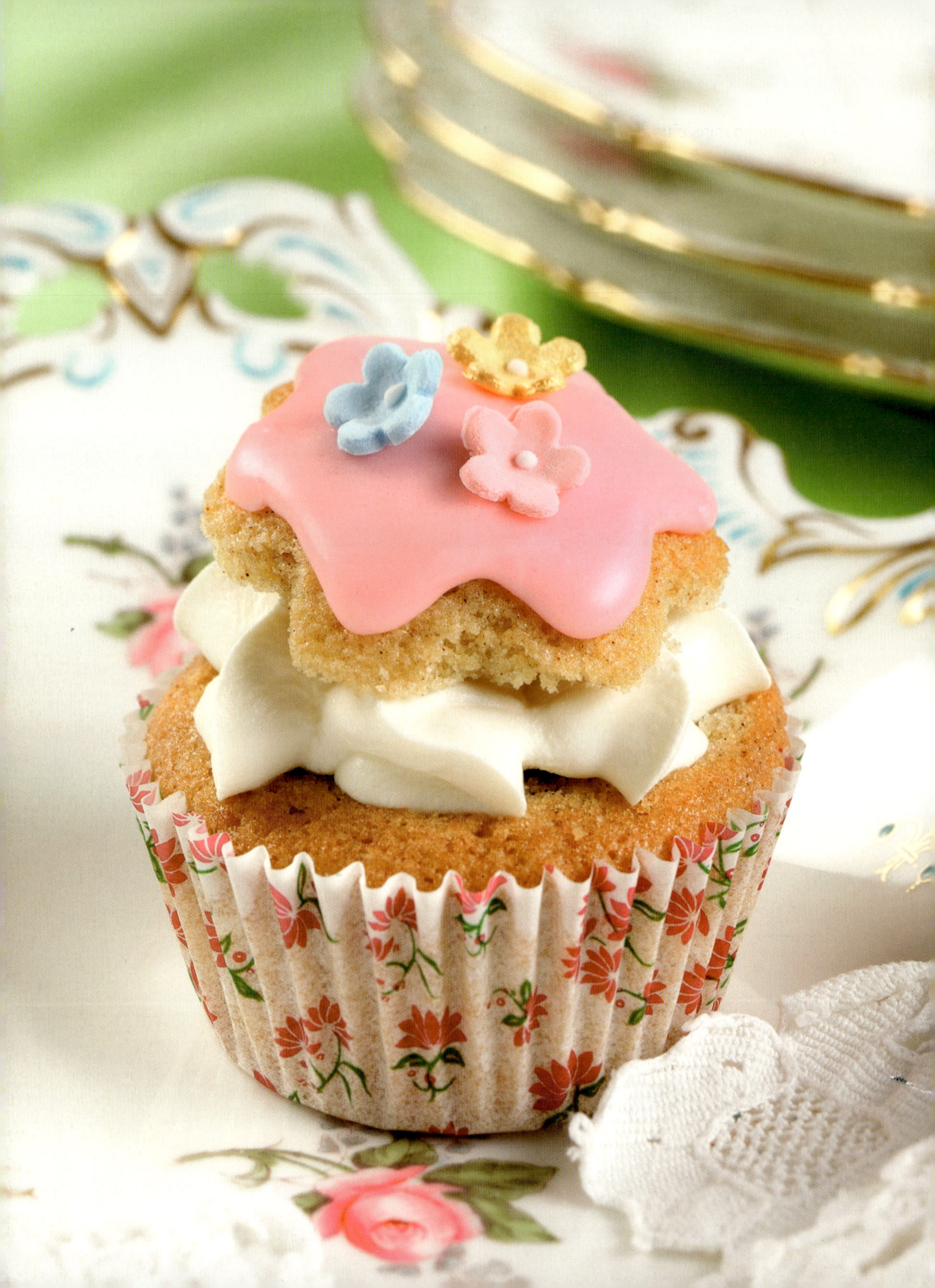

Makes 10
Prep time: 25 mins plus setting
Cook time: 16–18 mins

1 quantity Fairy Cupcake mixture, see page 27
2 tsp ground cinnamon
1 tsp finely grated lemon zest

TOPPING
150 g/5 oz ricotta cheese
75 g/2½ oz icing sugar
a few drops of pink food colouring
sugar flowers, to decorate

# Spring flower power cupcakes

1 Line a 10-hole cupcake pan with standard-size paper cases. Preheat the oven to 190°C/375°F/Gas 5.

2 Make up the Fairy Cupcake mixture as directed in steps 2 and 3 on page 27, then carefully stir in the ground cinnamon and lemon zest.

3 Spoon into the cake cases and bake for 16–18 minutes until lightly risen and lightly golden, and just firm to the touch. Transfer to a wire rack to cool.

4 For the topping, put the ricotta cheese in a piping bag fitted with a 1 cm/½ in star nozzle. Take a sharp knife and cut a circle off the top of each cake about 4 cm/1½ inch in diameter. Using either a small knife or flower-shaped cutter, form each sponge circle into a flower shape. Pipe a swirl of ricotta cheese on top of each of the cut cakes.

5 Sift the icing sugar into a small bowl and gradually mix in sufficient warm water to make a smooth, spreadable icing. Add a few drops of pink food colouring. Carefully spread each of the flower cut-out tops with pink icing and sit on top of each cupcake. Decorate with sugar flowers and allow to set.

Makes 16
Prep time: 50 mins plus chilling
Cook time: 33 mins (for cup cakes plus gingerbread)

FOR THE GINGERBREAD PEOPLE
125 g/4½ oz butter or margarine, softened
125 g/4½ oz dark brown sugar
1 large egg yolk
250 g/9 oz self-raising flour
1 tbsp ground ginger
assorted tubes of ready-made coloured piping icing
small sugar cake decorations

2 batches iced Sticky Toffee Cupcakes, see page 55

# Little party people cupcakes

1 Line 2 large baking sheets with baking parchment. Preheat the oven to 180°C/350°F/Gas 4.

2 To make the gingerbread people, in a mixing bowl, beat the butter or margarine with the sugar until paler and creamy-light in texture. Stir in the egg yolk.

3 Gradually sift in the flour and ginger, beating well after each addition, to form a soft, crumbly mixture. Bring the mixture together with your hands and gently knead it on a lightly floured work surface until smooth. Wrap and chill for at least 2 hours – preferably overnight.

4 Roll the dough out thinly on a lightly floured work surface. Using mini gingerbread people cutters, stamp out as many people as you can, re-rolling the dough as necessary. The mixture should make about 50. Arrange on the baking sheets, prick each with a fork and bake for about 8 minutes until lightly golden and just firm. Allow to cool on the baking sheets.

5 To serve, decorate each little person, stand one on top of each cupcake and serve the rest separately.

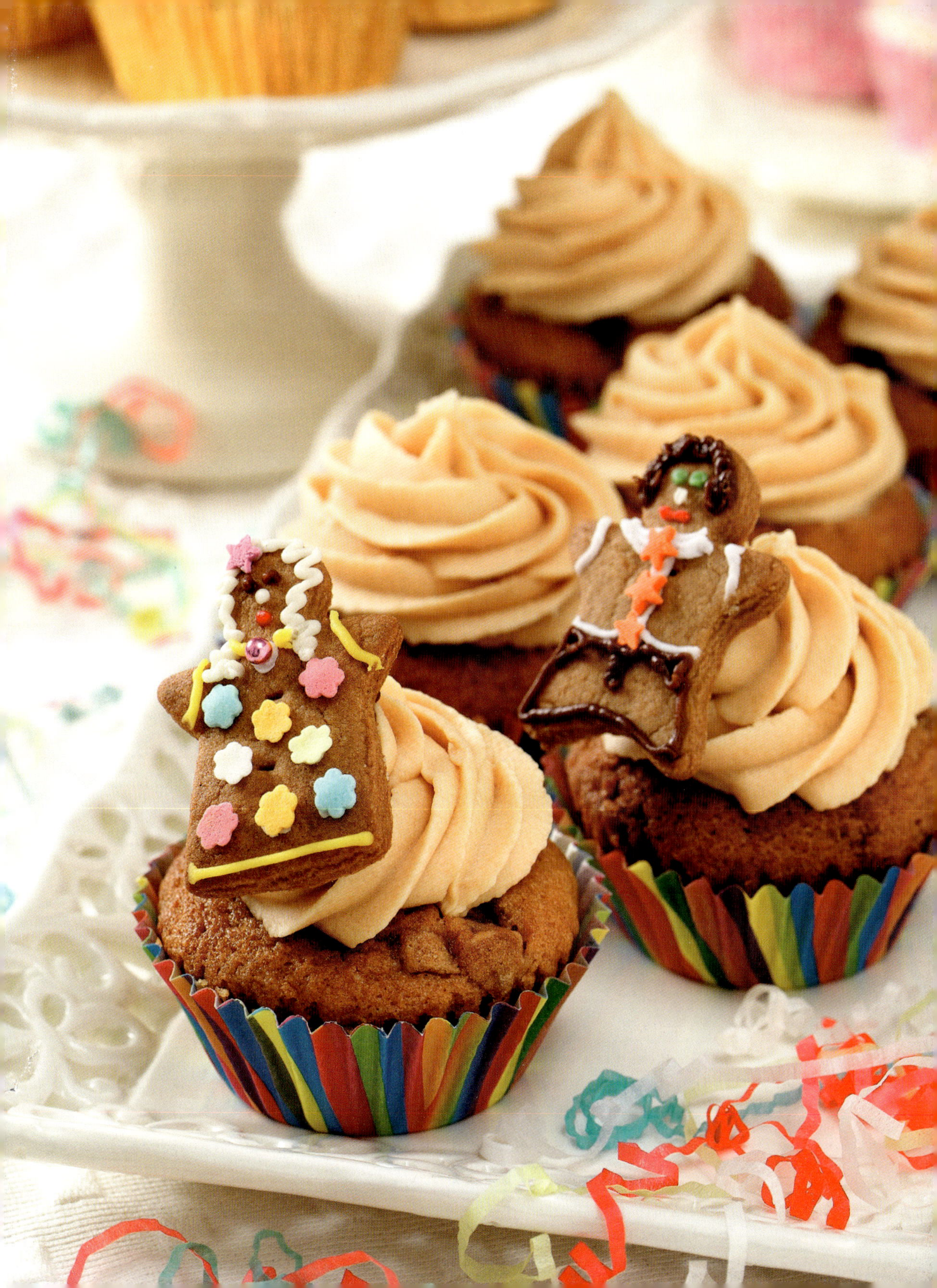

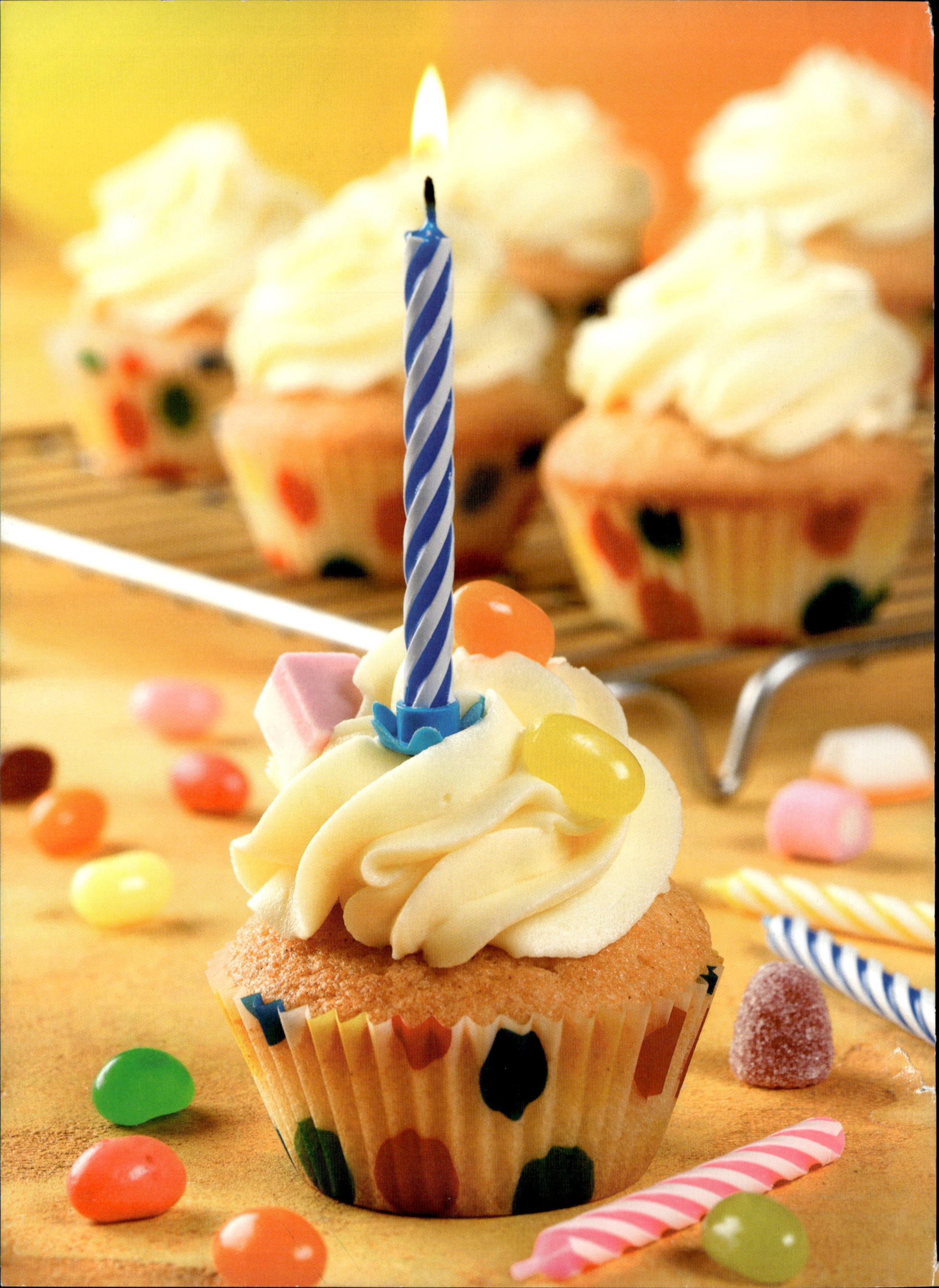

Makes 10
Prep time: 35 mins
Cook time: 16–18 mins

1 quantity Butterfly Cupcake mixture, see page 32

TOPPING
3 tbsp raspberry jam
1 quantity ganache-style icing made with white chocolate, see page 52
10 birthday cake candles
assorted mini sweets, such as Jelly Beans, Dolly Mixtures, to decorate

# Birthday cupcakes

1 Line a 10-hole cupcake pan with standard-size paper cases. Preheat the oven to 190°C/375°F/Gas 5.

2 Make up the Butterfly Cupcake mixture as directed in step 2 on page 32.

3 Spoon into the cake cases and bake for 16–18 minutes until lightly risen and lightly golden, and just firm to the touch. Transfer to a wire rack to cool.

4 Using a teaspoon, carefully scoop out a circle about 2 cm/$^3/_4$ in deep from the top of each cake and set aside. Spoon a little raspberry jam into each of the cakes and gently push the reserved sponge circle back on top.

5 Make up the white chocolate ganache as described in step 5 on page 52 and immediately spoon into a piping bag fitted with a 1 cm/$^1/_2$ in star nozzle and pipe a swirl on top of each cupcake. Note: once cool the icing will set firm.

6 Push a cake candle into the top of each cake and decorate with sweets before the ganache sets.

celebrations

Makes 12
Prep time: 30 mins plus setting
Cook time: 16–18 mins

115 g/4 oz butter or baking margarine, softened
115 g/4 oz caster sugar
115 g/4 oz pumpkin purée
2 eggs, beaten
115 g/4 oz wholemeal self-raising flour
2 tsp ground mixed spice

ICING
175 g/6 oz icing sugar
3–4 tsp orange juice
½ tsp finely grated orange zest
50 g/2 oz orange fondant icing

# Pumpkin pie cupcakes

1 Line a 12-hole cupcake pan with standard-size paper cases. Preheat the oven to 190°C/375°F/Gas 5.

2 In a mixing bowl, beat together the butter or margarine and sugar until pale and creamy. Mix in the pumpkin purée. Gradually whisk in the eggs, then sift the flour and spice on top, adding any husks that remain in the sieve. Using a large metal spoon, carefully fold the flour into the batter.

3 Spoon into the cake cases and bake for 16–18 minutes until lightly golden and just firm to the touch. Transfer to a wire rack to cool completely.

4 To ice, sift the icing sugar into a bowl and gradually mix in sufficient orange juice to make a smooth icing. Stir in the orange zest. Carefully spread the icing over each cake.

5 Roll out the fondant thinly on the work surface and cut out small pumpkin shapes with a sharp knife. Arrange on top of each cupcake. Allow to set for about 30 minutes.

**TIP**
To make pumpkin pureé, peel, deseed and dice pumpkin or squash. Place in a saucepan. Just cover with water and bring to the boil, then cover and simmer for 8–10 minutes until very tender. Drain well. Cool and mash.

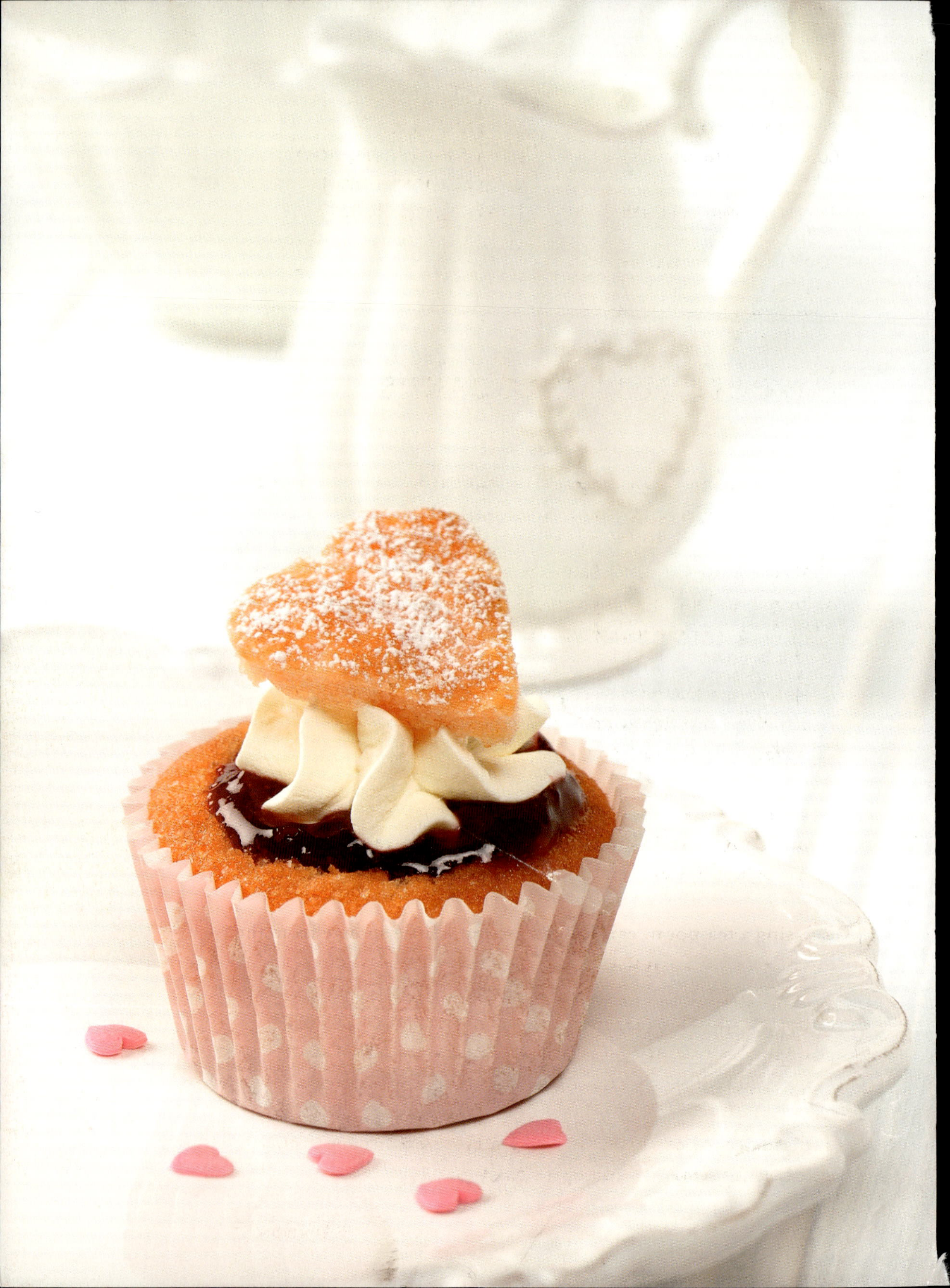

Makes 10
Prep time: 25 mins
Cook time: 16–18 mins

1 quantity Butterfly Cupcake mixture, see page 32
50 g/2 oz dried sour cherries, chopped
a few drops pink food colouring

TOPPING
5 tbsp cherry jam
150 ml/5 fl oz whipping cream
½ tsp pure almond extract
1 tbsp icing sugar, to dust

# Sweetheart cupcakes

1 Line a 10-hole cupcake pan with standard-size paper cases. Preheat the oven to 190°C/375°F/Gas 5.

2 Make up the Butterfly Cupcake mixture as directed in step 2 on page 32, then carefully stir in the chopped dried cherries and a few drops of pink food colouring.

3 Spoon into the cake cases and bake for 16–18 minutes until lightly risen and lightly golden, and just firm to the touch. Transfer to a wire rack to cool.

4 Take a sharp knife and cut a circle off the top of each cake about 4 cm/1½ in in diameter. Using either a small knife or heart-shaped cutter, form each sponge circle into a heart shape.

5 Using a teaspoon, carefully scoop out a little sponge from the top of each cake and fill with a little cherry jam.

6 Lightly whip the cream with the almond extract until just peaking. Transfer the cream to a piping bag fitted with a 1 cm/½ in star nozzle and pipe a swirl on top of each cake.

7 Sit the cake heart back on top of each cake at an angle; dust lightly icing sugar and serve straightaway.

celebrations

# Recipe index

Angelic lavender cupcakes 74
Birthday cupcakes 90
Blueberry muffins 18
Bramble, honey & oat muffins 60
Breakfast muesli & banana muffins 58
Butterfly cupcakes 32
Cappuccino cupcakes 44
Cherry almond cupcakes 30
Chocolate
    Chocolate fairy cupcakes 27
    Devil's food cupcakes 48
    Double chocolate muffins 20
    Easter animal parade cupcakes 84
    Mini Mayan gold cupcakes 52
    Mocha chestnut cupcakes 70
    Peanut butter & chocolate cupcakes 28
    White chocolate & pistachio muffins 38
Chocolate fairy cupcakes 27
Devil's food cupcakes 48
Double chocolate muffins 20
Easter animal cupcakes 84
Fairy cupcakes 26
Festive cranberry & marzipan muffins 82
Fresh coconut & lime cupcakes 46
Fruit
    Blueberry muffins 18
    Bramble, honey & oat muffins 60
    Breakfast muesli & banana muffins 58
    Cherry almond cupcakes 30
    Festive cranberry & marzipan muffins 82
    Fresh coconut & lime cupcakes 46
    Lemon & sultana muffins 22
    Lemon meringue cupcakes 50
    Orange & semolina muffins 64
    Raspberry "cranachan" muffins 40
    Seeded lemon cupcakes 70
Spiced apple sauce streusel muffins 24
Strawberry & fresh cream cupcakes 34
Goat's cheese & tomato muffins 62
Hot cross bun muffins 80
Lemon & sultana muffins 22
Lemon meringue cupcakes 50
Little party people cupcakes 88
Mexican corn bread muffins 68
Mini Mayan gold cupcakes 52
Mocha chestnut cupcakes 72
Nut
    Cherry almond cupcakes 30
    Mocha chestnut cupcakes 72
    Peanut butter & chocolate cupcakes 28
    Pecan & maple muffins 42
    White chocolate & pistachio muffins 38
Orange & semolina muffins 64
Partnership muffins 78
Peanut butter & chocolate cupcakes 28
Pecan & maple muffins 42
Pumpkin pie cupcakes 92
Raspberry "Cranachan" muffins 40
Savoury
    Goat's cheese & tomato muffins 62
    Mexican corn bread muffins 68
    Smoky bite-sized cheese & bacon muffins 66
Seeded lemon cupcakes 70
Smoky bite-sized cheese & bacon muffins 66
Spiced apple sauce streusel muffins 24
Spring flower power cupcakes 86
Sticky toffee cupcakes 54
Strawberry & fresh cream cupcakes 34
Sweetheart cupcakes 94
White chocolate & pistachio muffins 38

Acknowledgement

The author and publisher would like to thank 'Design A Cake' for supplying a selection of their paper cases for the muffins and cupcakes – see their website www.design-a-cake.co.uk for the full range.